Idolatry in the Pentateuch

Idolatry in the Pentateuch

An Innertextual Strategy

TRACY J. MCKENZIE

PICKWICK *Publications* · Eugene, Oregon

IDOLATRY IN THE PENTATEUCH
An Innertextual Strategy

Cascade Books
An Imprint of Wipf and Stock Publishers
199 W. 8th Ave., Suite 3
Eugene, OR 97401

www.wipfandstock.com

ISBN 13: 978-1-60608-607-0

Cataloging-in-Publication data:

McKenzie, Tracy J.

Idolatry in the Pentateuch : an innertextual strategy / Tracy J. McKenzie.

x + 138 p. ; 23 cm. — Includes bibliographical references.

ISBN 13: 978-1-60608-607-0

1. Bible. O.T. Exodus XXXII, 7–20—Criticism, interpretation, etc. 2. Bible. O.T. Deuteronomy IX, 12–21—Criticism, interpretation, etc. 3. Idolatry—Biblical teaching. 4. Bible—O.T. Pentateuch—Criticism, interpretation, etc. 5. Bible. O.T.—Theology. I. Title.

BS1199 L7 M36 2010

Manufactured in the U.S.A.

Contents

Acknowledgments

I WOULD LIKE TO thank my major professor, Dr. John Sailhamer, for his guidance in the completion of this work. His inspiring pursuit to understand the Hebrew Bible, his comprehension of the field of Old Testament studies, his thoughtful analysis, and his constant encouragement made the original dissertation possible.

I would also like to thank Dr. Bill Brown for reading the original dissertation and providing many helpful comments on it. His input over the final few months of that project was an encouragement to me. Furthermore, I would like to thank Dr. Vernon Steiner for his lasting influence upon me in teaching biblical Hebrew and for his input in an independent research seminar.

Although fellow students enriched my experience at Southeastern Baptist Theological Seminary through listening and interacting with ideas, I would like to thank one in particular. Dr. Joshua Williams and I spent hours together wrestling over ideas within Old Testament studies and translating sources. Moreover, his input in the final days of completion of the original dissertation made it a better project.

Finally and most important, I want to thank my wife, Beth, to whom this work is dedicated. Her selfless service to our family allowed me to complete the doctorate degree in a timely manner. She has only and always been a source of encouragement, patience, and wisdom during its course, and without her affection and friendship none of this would be possible.

Abbreviations

AnBib	Analecta Biblica
BDB	Brown, Francis, et al. *The Brown-Driver-Briggs Hebrew and English Lexicon.* Peabody, MA: Hendrickson, 1996
BETL	Bibliotheca ephemeridum theologicarum Lovaniensium
Bib	*Biblica*
BKAT	Biblischer Kommentar. Altes Testament
BZAW	Beihefte Zur Zeitschrift für die Alttestamentliche Wissenschaft
CahRB	Cahiers de la Revue biblique.
ConBOT	Coniectanea biblica: Old Testament Series
CCSL	Corpus Christianum: Series latina.
EvT	*Evangelische Theologie*
FC	Fathers of the Church (Washington, DC) 1947–
FRLANT	Forschungen Zur Religion und Literatur des Alten und Neuen Testaments
Int	*Interpretation*
JBL	*Journal of Biblical Literature*
JNSL	*Journal of Northwest Semitic Languages*
JSOTSup	Journal for the Study of the Old Testament: Supplement Series
NAC	New American Commentary
NCB	New Century Bible
NEchtB	Neue Echter Bibel
OBT	Overtures to Biblical Theology
OtSt	Oudtestamentische studiën
OTL	Old Testament Library
TRE	*Theologische Realenzyklopedie.* Edited by G. Krause and G. Müller. Berlin, 1977–

Abbreviations

UTB	Uni-Taschenbücher
SBET	*Scottish Bulletin of Evangelical Theology*
SBLSP	*Society for Biblical Literature Seminar Papers*
VT	*Vetus Testamentum*
VTSup	Supplements to Vetus Testamentum
WBC	Word Biblical Commentary
WTJ	Westminster Theological Journal
ZAW	*Zeitschrift für die alttestamentliche Wissenschaft*
ZTK	*Zeitschrift für Theologie und Kirche*

Introduction

THE RELEVANCE AND GOALS OF THE STUDY

The narrative of the golden calf relates the story of Israel's worship of a molten image. The story occurs in its most extensive accounts in two locations in the Old Testament. The first location is Exod 32:1–35. The second location is Deut 9:12–21. Scholars acknowledge that the report of the golden calf is important. The question that remains, however, is its significance for the Pentateuch. More precisely, what is the textual relationship between Exod 32:7–20 and Deut 9:12–21? What purpose does the relationship of these two texts of the golden calf play in understanding the compositional strategies within the Pentateuch?

Scholars have examined the narrative of the golden calf in connection with other parts of the Hebrew Bible.[1] Hans Christoph Schmitt, in an essay titled, "Die Erzählung vom Goldenen Kalb Ex. 32 und das Deuteronomistische Geschichtwerk," has said, "The literary-critical result of the narrative of the golden calf in Exod 32 is of central significance for the identification of the relationship between the Pentateuch and the Deuteronomistic History."[2] Schmitt's statement reveals that the relationship between Exodus 32 and Deuteronomy 9 has significance in determining the larger structure of the Hebrew Bible.[3]

The relationship of the golden calf narratives in Exodus 32 and Deuteronomy 9 may also have significance in determining the structure of the Pentateuch. An analysis of these texts in relationship to each other could provide evidence of compositional strategies within the Pentateuch. These strategies are often more conspicuous as one observes uneven syntax. Exodus 32 exhibits complexities within its syntax and structure. As a

---

1. Van Seters, *Life of Moses*, 290–318; Hyatt, *Commentary on Exodus*, 301–4; Hahn, *Das "Goldene Kalb,"* 140; Aurelius, *Fürbitter Israels*, 57–90.

2. Schmitt, "Erzählung vom Goldenen Kalb," 235.

3. Ibid., 242–46.

1

result, critical scholars have debated the presence of independent sources since the rise of historical criticism.[4] More traditional approaches attempt to explain the complexities within a presumed unity.[5]

The narrative of the golden calf within the book of Deuteronomy also presents a certain complexity. Scholarly works concerning this passage tend to concentrate in two divergent directions. They are inclined to focus either on its coherence within a Deuteronomic context or on its literary-critical relationship with Exodus.[6] In this manner, the relationship of Exodus 32 to Deuteronomy 9 has not gone unnoticed. Attempts to lay bare the relationship between the two often end in hypotheses concerning sources or a comparison of their respective dates. Each direction overlooks the relationship of these two passages in light of the final shape of the Pentateuch.

J. Clinton McCann affirms the direction of this project when he opens his article with the following statement: "Exod 32:1–14, along with the larger narrative which it introduces (Exod 32–34), is fundamental for understanding the Book of Exodus, the Pentateuch, the entire Old Testament, and indeed, the New Testament and the whole history of God's dealing with humanity."[7] This statement along with the view cited above by Schmitt not only indicate the importance of the incident of the golden calf narrated in Exod 32:7–20 but also the need for an examination of the other major textual unit dealing with the golden calf within the Pentateuch, Deut 9:12–21. An examination that explains the nature of the relationship between these two passages will aid a proper understanding of the Pentateuch and propose an understanding of the golden-calf narratives that coheres with the rest of the Bible.

The purpose of this analysis is to examine the relationship between the golden-calf texts of Exod 32:7–20 and Deut 9:12–21. It will argue that the two passages are part of an innertextual strategy making up the composition of the Pentateuch. The term *innertextuality* is understood as

---

4. Hahn, *"Goldene Kalb,"* 700–701.

5. See Rashi's comments concerning the complex makeup of punishments in the chapter in Rosenberg, *Shemoth,* 537; and Cassuto, *Commentary on the Book of Exodus,* 410.

6. For the former, see Zipor, "Deuteronomic Account of the Golden Calf," 20–33. For the latter, see Begg's articles concerning the destruction of the calf: Begg, "Destruction of the Calf," 208–51; and Begg, "Destruction of the Golden Calf Revisited," 469–79.

7. McCann, "Exodus 32:1–14," 277.

an intentional connection between narratives in order to combine them into a larger whole.[8] These connections are used to produce a structure through which an author[9] communicates a message.[10] While these connections between passages may be detected on various narrative levels, this analysis will focus on what Bar-Efrat labels the verbal level.[11]

The narratives in Exod 32:7–20 and Deut 9:12–21 are clearly related. The question is the nature of that relationship. Are the two units textually related? Is the relationship one of a late redaction of the Pentateuch, as many scholars have suggested? What role does the golden-calf narratives play in the composition of the Pentateuch? This work will demonstrate that the connection between Exod 32:7–20 and Deut 9:12–21 is directly related to the compositional strategy of the whole.

A SURVEY OF APPROACHES TO OLD TESTAMENT STUDIES FROM THE EIGHTEENTH CENTURY UNTIL THE PRESENT

Literary Criticism and the Objective of Old Testament Studies

The field of the Old Testament is in a state of transition. Since before the nineteenth century, scholars have attempted to uncover the makeup of the Old Testament through the discovery of literary layers and sources.[12] Emboldened by the literary criticism of Astruc, Eichhorn, and Wellhausen, they saw their task as to discover the historical progression associated with the Old Testament.[13] Each layer of tradition which was ascertained in the Old Testament, particularly the Pentateuch or Hexateuch, led to an examination of that layer. In his book *Die Biblische Urgeschichte: Redaktions- und Theologiegeschichtliche Beobachtungen zu Genesis 1,1—11,26*, Marcus Witte describes the development: "Hypotheses concerning the birth of

---

8. Sailhamer, *Old Testament Theology*, 209–12. This term will be explained in more detail below.

9. Throughout the book, I use the term *author* to signify a "composer" (see chapter 1 for more details) and not necessarily the more common modern view of author as a mere writer creating *ex nihilo*. Because of a distinction between composition and redaction, the term *redactor* is not to be preferred. See chapter 1 for a distinction between composition and redaction.

10. For a recent discussion of intentionality and speech acts, see Vanhoozer, *First Theology*, 159–203.

11. Bar-Efrat, "Observations on the Analysis of Structure," 154–73.

12. Wellhausen, *Prolegomena*, 6. See also Trattner, *Unravelling the Book of Books*.

13. See the preface by W. Robertson Smith in Wellhausen, *Prolegomena*, v–x.

the Pentateuch proliferated after the results of J. Astruc were confirmed by the examinations of Johann Gottfried Eichhorn, were proven to be on a solid scientific foundation, and were communicated to a larger research environment."[14] The scholarly interest in the production and growth of the Old Testament proliferated from there.

The complex makeup of the Pentateuch had been proposed since the seventeenth century.[15] Wellhausen focused scholarship on that makeup with his work *Prolegomena to the History of Ancient Israel*.[16] Wellhausen gained scholarly consensus due in part to the high opinion in which Old Testament scholarship held historical development.[17] He combined an attempt to understand the Pentateuch with an attempt to trace the historical milieu in which it was produced. In the introduction to his *Prolegomena to the History of Ancient Israel*, he states, "It is necessary to trace the succession of the three elements [sources] in detail, and at once to test and to fix each by reference to an independent standard, namely, the inner development of the history of Israel so far as that is known to us by trustworthy testimonies, from independent sources."[18] Wellhausen attempted to situate the preexistent sources in a historical period of the history of Israel.

Wellhausen accomplished this by examining the three "constituent elements" for a relationship to a period in Israel's history. The "constituent elements" were the Priestly Code, Deuteronomy, and the Jehovist.[19] His methodology and goal quickly became clear. He began his discussion with an attempt to isolate the notion of a singular place of worship. He states,

> But this oneness of the sanctuary in Israel was not originally recognized either in fact or in law; it was a slow growth of time. With the help of the Old Testament we are still quite able to trace the process. In doing so, it is possible to distinguish several stages of

14. Witte, *Biblische Urgeschichte*, 3.

15. Spinoza, *Theologico-Political Treatise*, 120–132. Another scholar in the seventeenth century who influenced critical scholars in the nineteenth century was Richard Simon. For a list of authors detailing Simon's contribution see Rogerson, *Old Testament Criticism*, 16.

16. Wellhausen, *Prolegomena*, 1–167, 392–410. See the survey by Thompson, *Century of Criticism*, 58.

17. Dillard and Longman, *An Introduction*, 40; Sandmel, "Haggada within Scripture," 105; Rogerson, *Old Testament Criticism*, 11.

18. Wellhausen, *Prolegomena*, 12.

19. Ibid.

development. We shall accordingly proceed to inquire whether the three constituent parts of the Pentateuch give tokens of any relationship to one or other of these; whether and how they fall in with the course of the historical development which we are able to follow by the aid of the historical and prophetic books from the period of the Judges onwards.[20]

This statement shows Wellhausen's purpose. He wanted to understand the connection between a "constituent element" and a period in history.

Wellhausen's success in *Prolegomena* won over the majority of scholars in his day. Scholarship focused its attention on the sources that made up the Old Testament. Witte evaluates this period by saying, "Consequently, the interests of research slipped to a survey of the pre-history of the Pentateuch, to the sources."[21] The primary focus of scholarship was no longer on the shape of the biblical text itself. The general objective of scholarship became an examination of those documents thought to constitute the Pentateuch and other biblical books. Rolf Rendtorff recognizes this movement in *The Canonical Hebrew Bible: A Theology of the Old Testament*. He writes, "It was, after all, an essential point of departure for modern historical-critical exegesis that the texts often appear to lack cohesion or are recognizably disparate, so that they seem to issue a veritable challenge to diachronic analysis and the discerning of earlier stages in their history of development. By devoting itself to this task, however, modern biblical criticism largely lost the present form of the text from view."[22] The importance of the shape of the biblical text disappeared in the wake of sources and strata within the text.

It was a respect for these sources and their original authors that led to a devaluation of any material not assigned to them. Because of the interest focused on the sources, an attempt to exegete the final shape lost relevance. Moreover, the one responsible for this final shape was seen in a negative light. Witte states, "Bound with the working out of the original sources, the moving of final redaction into the post-mosaic time and the with the interest on the 'pure,' 'original' texts, a devaluation took place since the end of the eighteenth century for the figure responsible for the end shape. The work of the final redactor appeared now as a distortion of the

---

20. Ibid., 18.

21. Witte, *Biblische Urgeschichte*, 3.

22. Rendtorff, *Canonical Hebrew Bible*, 2.

original clear narrative course of the sources."[23] Konrad Schmid assesses the loss of respect for the composer. He states, "Following the influence of Romanticism, the original author of the Old Testament writings—the Yahwist or Isaiah—was a religious genius while almost inevitably only the label of 'Epigone' remained for the one who completed it."[24] Since those responsible for the final shape were devalued, so was their work.

The work of those who composed the final shape of the text was seen as little more than inadequate editing. Rendtorff assesses the substandard opinion in which these authors were held. "In particular the authors of the text before us found themselves cast in the role of 'editors,' revisers, supplementers etc., who were considered of lesser value, and worthy of less attention, than the 'original' authors—despite the fact that in many cases the 'authors' are unknown or not traceable, or that, as in the case of the prophetic books, the composers of the 'original' words cannot generally be equated with the authors of the written texts."[25] This devaluation intensified a pursuit of the sources and theology of those sources that made up the Old Testament.

The role of the critical study of the Old Testament became an explanation of the sources and traditions that made up the Old Testament. A scholar was not primarily interested in what the final shape communicated but rather in the tradition underlying it. In an essay titled "Die Nachgeschichte alttestamentlicher Texte innerhalb des Alten Testaments," H. W. Hertzberg puts it bluntly: "It was not long ago when the interest in a passage which was considered artificial was essentially exhausted by merely explaining it as artificial. The text which was isolated held the interest. The magic word, gloss, gave the occasion to remove the doubtful verse from the task."[26] Rendtorff explains, "The present form of the text is generally accorded the least intrinsic value; rather, it is viewed as the result of 'secondary' and often not 'meaningful' . . . revision and reshaping. The previous, earlier, 'more original' stages of the text which are discerned in the analysis of the text, are given a higher rating."[27] The focus of study was on a text that had been stripped of any compositional activity.

23. Witte, *Biblische Urgeschichte*, 3–4.

24. Schmid, "Innerbiblische Schriftauslegung," 4.

25. Rendtorff, *Canonical Hebrew Bible*, 2.

26. Hertzberg, "Nachgeschichte alttestamentlicher Texte," 112.

27. Rendtorff, *Canonical Hebrew Bible*, 720.

Wellhausen was not the only scholar to significantly influence the discipline. Gunkel focused scholarship on the forms that constituted the text. Schmid discusses the connection between Wellhausen and Gunkel. In a manner similar to Wellhausen, Gunkel also pursued the individual writings detected in the text. These individual writings led him to the events to which the narratives referred, or to the different periods from which they stemmed. He subsequently sought the recurring forms in which the narratives were written.[28] Referring to Gunkel's form criticism, Thompson states, "[A] way back beyond written sources is opened up by this method."[29] Gunkel's method provided another means by which to pursue the prehistory of the final shape of the written text.

The activity of scholarship thus focused on the sources, forms, and traditions that made up the text. The final shape of the text was overlooked in order to pursue the objectives of literary and form criticism. So intense were these objectives that the goal of understanding the text in its present shape was practically forgotten. Thus Rolf Rendtorff, in 1976, could say of the text comprising the Sinai pericope, "The research has certainly sorted out some components, especially different legal codes; but how that entirety has come together and additionally, the question whether or not determined, recognizable intentions and guiding principles are at work has hardly even been asked."[30] The Sinai pericope lies at the heart of the Pentateuch. Yet the theological message intended in it had been overlooked due to other pursuits.

Schmid also notes the lack of interest in the final shape of the Pentateuch during these years. In his article, he states, "The fact that the sources had been bound together by redactors was undisputed. How was this redactional activity to be grasped, or to be determined, or to be described? One would expect the question to be asked and yet it hardly was.[31] Scholarly discussion did include the notion of redactional bridges between the sources. Yet the conversation among critical scholars rarely turned towards a description of the final shape. Schmid continues, "The interest of the research laid with the source writings as such . . ."[32]

28. Schmid, "Innerbiblische Schriftauslegung," 5.
29. Thompson, *Century of Criticism*, 110.
30. Rendtorff, *Überlieferungsgeschichtliche Problem*, 25.
31. Schmid, "Innerbiblische Schriftauslegung," 6.
32. Ibid.

Hertzberg also noted that there was a lack of interest in the author of the entire Pentateuch. In a 1952 article, he states, "A book concerning the author of the whole, the final redactor, still lacks full validity."[33] The focus of scholarship was still not on the final shape of the biblical books.

More traditional scholars also noticed the dominant trend in Old Testament scholarship. In the preface of his commentary on Exodus, Cassuto noted his own agenda in contrast with others.

> The commentaries written in our generation on any book of the Pentateuch are, in most instances, chiefly devoted to investigating the sources and to determining the process by which they have been fitted together. They annotate the documentary fragments that they discern in the book rather than the book itself. The great importance attached by exegetes to the question of the sources diverts their attention from the study of the work that has grown out of these documents. In their opinion, the study of the sources takes precedence over that of the book as we have it. To my mind, the reverse view is the more reasonable . . . at no time have I lost sight of the fact that my main task was to explain the book before us.[34]

Cassuto recognized the objective of most scholars. He attempts, rather, to explain the book in its present shape. Others have recently focused their attention in a similar direction.

The Shift in Old Testament Studies

PROPHETIC STUDIES

The shift in direction in Old Testament studies did not happen instantaneously. Nor did it happen unilaterally. The transition occurred over many years and in different branches of Old Testament studies. Scholars in the prophetic literature began to see the interpretive nature of the prophetic books. In the recent past, prophetic literature had been examined in order to hear the very words of the prophets and enter into their world.[35] The intent was to examine their message as it was given to their audience. Any additions to their words were considered spurious. These secondary ad-

---

33. Hertzberg, "Ist Exegese Theologisch Möglich?" 111; quoted in Schmid, "Innerbiblische Schriftauslegun," 6.

34. Cassuto, *Commentary on the Book of Exodus*, 1.

35. Seitz, "On Letting a Text 'Act Like a Man,'" 151–58; Schmid, "Innerbiblische Schrift-auslegung," 9.

ditions were to be detected and discounted while importance was placed on the very words of the prophets.

George Adam Smith, in the preface to his commentary on the Twelve, reveals this perspective. Smith offers an unfavorable review of the excesses of critical scholarship concerning the Minor Prophets. Too many passages were being emended or excised without adequate justification. Scholars were eliminating words they considered secondary to the actual words of the prophets. To Smith this meant that the prophets were not allowed to speak. Among other things, the result was a "depreciation of the spiritual insight and foresight of pre-exilic writers."[36] Smith was concerned because his goal involved hearing the prophets' own words. He did not want any words to be unnecessarily excised but rather to enter the prophetic world. A change was coming, however, which would put a greater focus on the textual nature of the prophetic message.

Gerhard von Rad signaled this change in attitude, which would soon become evident. In the second volume of his *Old Testament Theology*, von Rad dealt with the prophets. Von Rad directed attention to the interpretive process involved in the prophetic books and discussed the influence of this aspect in a books' formation.[37] A prophetic book was not a bare recording of the prophet's oracles. Instead, different types of literature were involved.[38] Stories were told about the individual prophet and his world along with the prophet's oracles. These different literary forms were gathered into "little complexes."[39] These complexes could also take on a larger shape. Larger arrangements, for which von Rad could recognize no principle of organization, involved "the formation of more elaborate complexes, that is to say, where it is a case of the collection of collections."[40] These complexes or larger collections revealed an interpretive process in the authoring of the prophetic books.

These characteristics of prophetic books would eventually require scholars to incorporate them into the process of exegesis. The implications of von Rad's discussion seem even more central to the development within Old Testament studies that focuses on the final shape of the

---

36. Smith, *Book of the Twelve*, ix–xi.
37. Schmid, "Innerbiblische Schriftauslegung," 9.
38. Von Rad, *Old Testament Theology*, 33–35.
39. Ibid., 39.
40. Ibid., 40.

text. These complexes were to speak to a later generation other than its originally oral audience. Von Rad understood that the words of a prophet could be recast from the original situation to that of a literary context.[41] This recasting involved the collection of stories and oracles of a prophet into a written context. This new context demanded its own interpretive boundaries in addition to the social world of the prophet.

Von Rad writes concerning a passage in Isaiah: "What gives the passage its great interest is that it shows how in certain circumstances the prophet broke the connection between his words and their original hearers and, without the slightest alteration, carried the message over to apply to hearers and readers of a more distant future."[42] This was an innovative notion in prophetic studies. The written complexes that reiterated the prophetical oracles were not intended for the original audience but for a later readership. It is only as one isolated the forms or units, discerned the activity that joined the units into a complex, and understood the purpose that motivated the arrangement that he *hears* the written text.

In order to appreciate these written complexes, scholarship had to overcome its single-minded focus on the very words of the prophets. According to von Rad, only then would exegetes gain a new perspective into the prophetic message. He states, "The way in which tradition mounts and grows can be closely followed in the prophetic writings. Exegesis must be less ready than at present [sic] to look on this infusion of new blood into the prophetic tradition as 'spurious' or an unhappy distortion of the original."[43] Von Rad saw that scholarship was overlooking an important component of prophetic studies.

In the closing paragraph of the section, von Rad challenges his contemporaries to consider another aspect of the prophetic books. "Present-day exegesis is concerned above all else to discover the content of each specific oracle as it was understood by the prophet himself. But, while not abandoning this effort, ought it not perhaps to be more aware that this is only one possible way among many of understanding an oracle ... Ought we not also to remember that when a prophecy came into the hands of those who transmitted the traditions, this itself meant that the time when the prophecy could be taken in the strict sense which it had when it was

41. Ibid., 39–46.
42. Ibid., 43.
43. Ibid., 46; quoted in Schmid, "Innerbiblische Schriftauslegung," 9.

originally delivered was already a thing of the past?"[44] Von Rad recognized that prophetic studies had overlooked the literary context in order to focus on the prophetic personality. His insight ultimately helped to guide a new generation of scholars to a solution.

STUDIES RELATED TO INTERPRETIVE TECHNIQUES WITHIN THE OLD TESTAMENT

Another branch of Old Testament studies in which the pursuit of sources and prophetic personalities was challenged relates to exegetical techniques within the writings themselves. I. L. Seeligmann initiated this move in an article titled "Voraussetzungen der Midraschexegese."[45] Von Rad had actually referred to Seeligmann's article in the closing pages of his chapter concerning the move from oral to written prophecy.[46] Among the various phenomena that Seeligmann demonstrated is a reuse of literary units within the Old Testament.[47] These literary units recur in various locales within the Old Testament or in some other ancient document. These repeated or reused written literary units illustrate a literary and interpretive framework within the Old Testament.[48] This interpretive framework provided a literary context from which to understand a passage.

Seeligman points out in his opening paragraph that his contemporaries operated in a manner that isolated a text to its original historical milieu. This practice created a distance between the exegete and the text. In contrast, Seeligmann attempted to show that there existed within the Old Testament itself an exegesis of previously written texts. This exegesis within the Old Testament utilized written texts and commented on them. Through word play and the adaptation of narratives, the biblical texts received their shape.[49] Thus the biblical texts were fitted for a particular instance and eventually solidified into the canon.[50] His demonstration of an interpretive process within the biblical texts helped show that an ap-

44. Von Rad, *Old Testament Theology*, 48–49.

45. Seeligmann, "Voraussetzungen der Midraschexegese." See also Sandmel, "Haggada within Scripture."

46. Von Rad, *Old Testament Theology*, 48.

47. Seeligmann, "Voraussetzungen Der Midraschexegese," 152–57.

48. Ibid. Cf. Sandmel, "Haggada within Scripture," 106–15. Sandmel sees the different narratives as "haggadic recastings of a single source."

49. Seeligmann, "Voraussetzungen der Midraschexegese," 167.

50. Ibid., 152.

proach to interpretation was needed that took into account the shape of the biblical texts themselves.

Although occurring later, Michael Fishbane's work called *Biblical Interpretation in Ancient Israel* also demonstrated the interpretive makeup of biblical texts.[51] Fishbane's model involves the growth of textual material through exegesis. Fishbane understood that different groups read the received texts and supplemented those texts with notations. The various groups supplemented the text for different reason, but the result was an accumulation of textual material. The distinct accretions can be discerned through criteria that demonstrate the accumulation.

Fishbane lists several criteria he uses to discern an interpretive comment. The criteria involve technical formulae that indicate a comment on another passage, comparing parallel texts within or between the Masoretic tradition or a version of it, and certain redundant features of texts—whether they be terms, phrases, or variants.[52] For Fishbane, these criteria suggest a particular reason for the formation of the text in each instance.

Fishbane discusses four categories of biblical notation, which he calls innerbiblical exegesis.[53] What is important for this survey, however, is Fishbane's influence upon scholarship. His work *Biblical Interpretation in Ancient Israel* demonstrated within the Old Testament itself that an interpretive process was active in shaping the biblical texts. For Fishbane, the process involved glosses or interpretations, i.e., innerbiblical exegesis, which attempts to explain the text in question. Scribes and others have taken the authoritative text (*traditum*) and commented upon those texts (*traditio*) resulting in a certain shaping of the canonical texts.

Along with Seeligmann and Fishbane, Sandmel and others showed an interpretive process present in the texts of the Old Testament.[54] This interpretive process resulted in the accumulation and congealment of biblical material. One is able to discern this process by means of the glosses and the reuse of material by those who made the notations. This

---

51. Fishbane, *Biblical Interpretation*.

52. Ibid., 42–43, 291.

53. Some have suggested that Fishbane is anachronistically reading later rabbinic categories of interpretation onto the biblical data. Van Seters, "Redactor in Biblical Studies," 16.

54. Schmid, "Innerbiblische Schriftauslegung," 10, notes various scholars and their work in this area.

view of the production of the biblical texts led these scholars to examine the shape of the texts in order to understand the development of those texts. They differed with the previous generations of scholars in the objective of their examinations. They were not examining sources or strata; rather, they were looking for an interpretive process discernible in the final shape.

The Influence of Form, Oral, and Tradition Criticism

Another sign of transition in Old Testament studies was the rise of form, oral, and tradition criticism. While Wellhausen was gaining the attention of Old Testament scholarship with his literary criticism, Hermann Gunkel was examining the prehistory of the written sources.[55] Although Gunkel agreed with certain features of Wellhausen's program, he thought that knowing the four sources was insufficient. In contrast, he proposed an agenda that would uncover the origins of individual textual units found within those sources.[56] While much Old Testament scholarship was focused on the four sources, Gunkel attempted to uncover the form and life setting of these individual stories which made up the Pentateuch. He wrote:

> A new and fundamental question is: What unit is really the constituent unit in Genesis, the one which we should first apply ourselves to? For there are a number of different units in Genesis. The most comprehensive unit is the whole Pentateuch, then Genesis, and then the single collections of legends that preceded it; then the individual legends of which the book was composed . . . All of these various units must be considered. But the first question is, Which of these units is most important for our purposes, that is, which of them was the original unit in oral tradition? . . . For the proper understanding of Genesis, also, it is of critical importance that this question be clearly met and correctly answered.[57]

Gunkel sought the original form of the stories contained in Genesis. How were these stories from Genesis passed down? Were they adapted from an oral form? What were their most basic forms? From what life setting did it arise? After answering these questions, Gunkel would then

---

55. Gunkel, *Legends of Genesis*; Gunkel and Zimmern, *Schöpfung und Chaos*, 5–6.

56. From the perspective of a text's origin, Gunkel also highlighted the prehistory of the text's incorporation into a larger unit. See p. 7 above.

57. Gunkel, *Legends of Genesis*, 42–43.

consider how these individual stories were combined into a complex or a cycle of narratives.[58]

Gunkel's proposals introduced doubt into the findings of literary criticism. A radical break was proposed in a 1959 paper read by Ivan Engnell.[59] Engnell chided those who still based their research on the findings of the Wellhausenian school of literary criticism. From Engnell's point of view, such a method had been outdated by the early findings of form criticism and the developing methodology of the tradition-historical method. In his view, the tradition-historical method (that is, the notion that the Old Testament was the product of the oral tradition process) was not based on outdated literary-critical methods but on new analyses of the role of oral tradition in the field of comparative religion. [60]

Although literary criticism had provided the foundation for biblical studies for a century or more, Engnell advocated a fundamental break. "I would like to state then, that the break with the literary-critical method must be radical; no compromise is possible."[61] Engnell viewed the study of the Old Testament from a fundamentally different basis compared to previous scholarship. At the time, Engnell's position must have appeared overstated.[62] Gunkel had initiated a program, however, that would weaken the foundation of source criticism.

In 1976, Rolf Rendtorff's, *Das überlieferungsgeschicte Problem des Pentateuch* further undermined the foundation of source criticism.[63] In it, Rendtorff demonstrated how major tradition complexes provide the large narrative units to the Pentateuch. He traced one such unit from Genesis 12 to 50 by identifying a promise theme woven throughout the unit.[64] If this was part of a source that runs throughout the Pentateuch (the Yahwist for

---

58. Gunkel, *Genesis*, xxiii–lxxxvi.

59. Engnell, "Methodological Aspects of Old Testament Study," 13–30.

60. For a distinction between the Scandinavian school of tradition history and the German school, see Rendtorff, "Traditio-Historical Method and the Documentary Hypothesis," 5.

61. Engnell, "Methodological Aspects of Old Testament Study," 21.

62. Rendtorff, "Literarkritik und Traditionsgeschichte," 138–53.

63. Rendtorff, *Das überlieferungsgeschichtliche Problem*. To grasp his evolution of thought, read the foreword in *Das überlieferungsgeschichte Problem* and compare his article "Literarkritik und Traditionsgeschichte," 138–53 with his paper "Traditio-Historical Method and the Documentary Hypothesis," 5–11.

64. Rendtorff, *Überlieferungsgeschichtliche Problem*, 29–75; Rendtorff, "'Yahwist' as Theologian," 2–9.

example), should not this all-encompassing promise theme be discernible later in the Pentateuch within this same source? The fact that this was not the case had repercussions for the Documentary Hypothesis. The Documentary Hypothesis, with its premise of four original sources woven throughout the Pentateuch, could no longer be sustained. Rendtorff himself states, "The assumption of 'sources' in the sense of the documentary hypothesis can no longer make any contribution today to the understanding of the formation of the Pentateuch."[65] That statement, and the basis from which it was made, has had far reaching consequences for pentateuchal criticism.[66]

READING THE TEXT AS A UNITY

Another factor causing transition in Old Testament studies was the notion of reading a text as a unit. Classic literary criticism noticed disturbances or complexities in the linguistic forms of a passage. These complexities pointed to divisions within the text, resulting in a fractured text. Rendtorff assesses the impact of literary criticism: "Its first concern is with the question of the 'literary unity or lack of unity' of the text, and to start with in regard to the 'individual text.' In the case of 'revelation of breaks, unevenness or tensions' an attempt is then made to ascribe the 'text parts obtained' to 'meaningful sequences in narrative and action' and then to set them 'in broader—again meaningful—contexts' (quotations from Schmidt 1991, 120). With this procedure, in each case a new text is 'reconstructed,' which implies that the present final text at least is not meaningful."[67]

This preoccupation with the individual pieces resulted in a fractured view of the Old Testament books and canon. A change occurred, however, that shifted the focus of interpretation to the boundaries of a literary work, regardless of tensions or complexities. Some have suggested that literary theories from the disciplines of literature and linguistics were the cause for the change within Old Testament studies.[68] Certainly scholars had been influenced by the progression of literary theory, but the pre-

65. Rendtorff, *Das überlieferungsgeschichtliche Problem*, 148; Rendtorff, "Yahwist As Theologian," 8.

66. For the state of current pentateuchal research as it reacted to Rendtorff's challenge, see Wynn-Williams, *State of the Pentateuch*, 3, in particular, note 1.

67. Rendtorff, *Canonical Hebrew Bible*, 719.

68. Barton, *Reading the Old Testament*, 153–79.

cise dimension of that influence is still in question. Eventually this focus on the individual sources gave way to a more unified reading of biblical books.[69]

The goal of scholarship progressed from the individual sources to the entire unit, from the pieces to the whole of the biblical text. The whole shape was often seen as the canonical texts. This can be illustrated in Childs's work *Biblical Theology in Crisis*.[70] His proposal for a new biblical theology attempted to use the canon as the proper context. Childs acknowledges that theological concerns compelled him to consider the canon as an appropriate context.[71] One must also consider, however, the significance that literary theory played upon his proposal to do canonical theology. In his discussion of different contexts from which to interpret the text, the theoretical "newer criticism" seems to have had an impact. He writes, "It is also true, as the adherents to the school of 'newer criticism' in the field of English literature have continued to point out, that an interpreter can approach the same material and use only the final stage of the literature as a legitimate context."[72] This statement by Childs indicates the growing movement in academic circles that an interest in the final stage of a text was an appropriate context from which to interpret that text.

The Lack of Consensus in Source Criticism

The disparity among the results of literary criticism also contributed to disillusionment with it as a basis for Old Testament studies. Literary criticism had attempted to delineate sources for over a century. Scholarship still had no definitive solution for the demarcation and time frame of the different sources.[73] Although this critique had been leveled before, it was not until the prolonged passage of time that this inability began to exert influence.[74] In order to deal with the data, additional sources, strata, or distinct redactions had to be postulated.

---

69. For this development, see Thiselton, *New Horizons in Hermeneutics*, 89–90, 471–95.

70. Childs, *Biblical Theology in Crisis*, 1–87.

71. Ibid., 99.

72. Ibid., 98.

73. See Thompson, *Moses and the Law*, 104–5, 164–65 where he discusses the issues of the makeup and time frame of P. See also Rendtorff, *Überlieferungsgeschichtliche Problem*, 80–146.

74. Archer, *Survey of Old Testament Introduction*, 73–95. Archer seemingly represents a traditional critique that did not carry much weight outside evangelicalism.

From this point of view R. N. Whybray levels one of his critiques of source criticism and the Documentary Hypothesis: "Subsequent modifications of the Documentary Hypothesis have not increased its plausibility. The postulation of additional documents, which are of limited scope, marks the breakdown of a hypothesis which is essentially one of *continuous* documents running through the Pentateuch. Attempts to make the hypothesis more flexible by speaking rather vaguely of 'strata' and the like rather than of documents are essentially denials of a purely literary hypothesis."[75] Whybray speaks here of the differing opinions among scholars as to what actually constituted the different sources. If little agreement exists over the parameters of the four independent documents, then the theory eventually weakens.

The methodological difficulty but interpretive importance of the dating of texts only heightened the lack of consensus. Rendtorff points to this factor when he says, "While previously, at least in German-speaking circles, it was possible to speak, almost without fear of challenge, of a 'Yahwist' situated in the early period of the monarchy, who formed the basis for the theological interpretation of the Pentateuch, today it is frequently disputed that it is possible to establish substantial continuous 'sources' in the Pentateuch . . ."[76] Without methodological precision, the dating differed among scholars. This methodological imprecision only frustrated the efforts at interpretive understanding and agreement since interpretation was dependent upon understanding the historical milieu from which a source arose.

PENTATEUCHAL STUDIES

Alongside these developments in Old Testament studies in general came innovative works in the area of pentateuchal studies. In what Schmid calls a "pioneering work,"[77] H. C. Schmitt demonstrates a faith theme woven throughout the Pentateuch by means of a "terminus technicus."[78] In an article, "Redaktion des Pentateuch im Geiste der Prophetie, Beobachtungen zur Bedeutung der 'Glaubens'—Thematik innerhalb der Theologie des Pentateuch," Schmitt examines the Pentateuch as a whole. He writes,

---

75. Whybray, *Making of the Pentateuch*, 130–31.

76. Rendtorff, *Canonical Hebrew Bible*, 721.

77. Schmid, "Innerbiblische Schriftauslegung," 13.

78. Schmitt, "Redaktion des Pentateuch," 175.

> If one takes seriously the model concerning the origin of the deuteronomistic history as a point of orientation for a new approach to the literary problem of the Pentateuch, then one must also take as a starting point for the Pentateuch redactions which span the entire work and only pursue the treatment of redactional relationships of alleged sources and blocks of tradition. Here, as did Rendtorff, one is able to take as a starting point the currently existing form of the tradition complexes and from its structure pursue the theological intentions shaping it.[79]

Although he was not the first scholar in recent history to call attention to the final shape, Schmitt's work is pioneering, in part, because it takes seriously the present shape of the Pentateuch, proceeding from that shape to find the theological intentions contained therein.

Schmitt finds these intentions because of the theological imprints left on the final shape. He examines the whole of the Pentateuch for passages that exhibit a similar imprint. This association of passages due to similar features demonstrates an interpretive innovation and provides another reason why Schmitt's work is pioneering. This examination of passages connected through linguistic features involves texts placed in relationship to one another; thus, the interplay of texts with one another forms the basis for interpretation.

Another important result of Schmitt's work is the profile of the final shape of the Pentateuch. Schmitt concludes that a faith theme evinces a temporal factor. It cuts across Priestly and non-Priestly material, subsequently showing a post-priestly redaction. He states, "This result from Num 20:1–13 is now, in this respect, of particular importance as it provides a first clue for the temporal position of the redaction introducing the faith theme in the Pentateuch."[80] Schmitt calls attention to the faith theme that spans the alleged sources of the Documentary Hypothesis and shows that the redaction of the priestly material was not the final edition of the Pentateuch.

Schmitt traces the passages evincing this faith theme through terminological relationships, syntactical structure (*Hiphil* of אמן plus ב), and the form found in other "faith" passages.[81] In doing so, he demonstrates

---

79. Ibid., 172–73.
80. Ibid., 180–81.
81. Ibid., 183.

a structure that shows a theological imprint. This imprint is distributed throughout the Pentateuch and demonstrates compositional activity.[82]

More recently, Marcus Witte has produced another important monograph within pentateuchal studies. In his book *Die biblische Urgeschichte: Redaktions- und theologiegeschichtliche Beobachtungen zu Genesis 1,1—11,26,* Witte examines the final redaction in Gen 1–11. He states, "We concentrate, rather, on the description of the theology of the final redaction and on the survey of the literary and theological critical background of possible texts of the final redaction."[83] Witte's monograph marks a new point in Pentateuch and Old Testament studies. Commenting on Witte's monograph, Schmid writes, "Only in recent times was he [the redactor] the object of a monograph."[84] In a manner similar to Schmitt's article, Witte's interest in the final redaction of Genesis 1–11 separates him from other scholars. Witte pursues the theology contained in the final shaping of the primeval history. Others had written on the redactional stages and layers of pentateuchal texts, and Witte utilized redaction criticism as well. Witte initiated a new objective in critical scholarship, however, because he aimed to describe the theology in the final shape of the text.

In a 1981 essay "Die Eigenständigkeit der Urgeschichte. Ein Beitrag zur Diskussion um den 'Jahwisten,'" Frank Crüseman reveals the changing attitudes about the objectives of Old Testament studies. He states, "The final redaction lying before us is to be taken seriously theologically and historically. That is certainly a task with which Old Testament studies has even yet hardly been concerned."[85] This statement illustrates the transition in Old Testament studies.

An Objective of Contemporary Old Testament Studies

The objective of Old Testament scholarship in the twentieth century diverged widely. This situation appears to be changing. In his monograph on Genesis 1–11, Marcus Witte makes this statement after reviewing pentateuchal scholarship: "Approaches to a literature and theological-historical

---

82. According to Fohrer, a distribution of features throughout an entire work constitutes composition. Fohrer, *Exegese des Alten Testaments,* 145–47.

83. Witte, *Biblische Urgeschichte,* 47.

84. Schmid, "Innerbiblische Schriftauslegung," 7.

85. Crüseman, "Eigenständigkeit der Urgeschichte," 14; quoted in Witte, *Biblische Urgeschichte,* 47.

classification and assessment of the final redaction occur in the context of all presently supported, historical-critically argued pentateuchal models."[86] In another point of his summary of research, Witte comments, "The present perception is to appreciate the final redaction compositionally and theologically in connection with the focus in pentateuchal research on the whole entirety."[87] For Witte, the final redaction holds a place of central importance when focused on an understanding of the entire Pentateuch. This brief sketch of scholarship has attempted to show a growing focus on the final shape as an important locus of compositional and theological insight.

The Pentateuch is not the only text of the Old Testament receiving this attention. The canon of the Old Testament has also received the interest of scholarship. In the opening of his book *The Canonical Hebrew Bible: A Theology of the Old Testament*, Rolf Rendtorff states, "The Old Testament is a theological book."[88] This statement may initially appear peculiar. The fact that Rendtorff makes it indicates the transition in the aim of Old Testament scholarship in recent history. Rendtorff continues by explaining the different approaches that have been the foundation for studies within the Old Testament. He then highlights von Rad's canonical presentation in von Rad's two-volume work, *Old Testament Theology*. Rendtorff is not satisfied, however, and says, "The present book follows this approach, but develops it a step further, not only assuming the canonical basis of the Hebrew Bible but also making the texts themselves, in the present 'canonical shape,' the point of departure for the account."[89] Rendtorff goes beyond a mere canonical presentation of his research. His research is based on the canonical texts themselves.

Rendtorff resumes discussing the foundation for his theology: "This interpretation of the texts occurs within the context of historical-critical biblical research. It goes a step beyond the methodological approaches in widespread current use by following to its end the path of transmission that has emanated in the present shape of the text and by *focusing its primary attention* on this final form. Diachronic aspects are certainly not ignored; however, essentially they are considered in relation to the

---

86. Witte, *Biblische Urgeschichte*, 45.

87. Ibid., 45–46.

88. Rendtorff, *Canonical Hebrew Bible*, 1.

89. Ibid.

contribution they may make to the understanding of the texts in their present, final, form."[90] Rendtorff provides a careful beginning to his *The Canonical Hebrew Bible: A Theology of the Old Testament*. His statement explains that the basis for his theology is the text of the Old Testament in its current shape.

The previous review shows that critical scholarship has made a determined shift toward the final shape of the biblical text. A central objective is an examination of the theology of the Old Testament in its current shape. An appreciation has even developed for authors in the past whose objective was an explanation of that canonical shape. In a review of the new edition of the 1878 Old Testament commentary series by C. F. Keil and Franz Delitzsch, H. C. Schmitt comments that the authors' aim was to, "explain the content of divine revelation both factually and truthfully not only through a grammatical-historical manner but at the same time to develop it in a biblical-theological manner."[91] It is Schmitt's next statement that suggests the shift that has taken place. He says, "This [aim] is valid above all in light of the stronger emphasis on the redaction-critical question in the most recent phase of Old Testament studies. Currently, a more intensive effort for an understanding of the final shape of the Pentateuch exists for which pentateuchal commentaries which did not follow the Documentary Hypothesis generated worthwhile discussion from out of the middle of the last century."[92] This statement indicates the valuable insights of commentaries not driven by the Documentary Hypothesis. Furthermore, this statement demonstrates a new attitude toward a holistic approach to the Pentateuch and the Old Testament in general.

Innerbiblical Exegesis and Allusion

In light of the developments in the study of the Old Testament, new proposals are being made that contribute to Old Testament scholarship. Schmitt's examination based on the association of passages that exhibit similarities is an example of such a proposal. These proposals have to do with the relationship of one text to another. Proposals involving this notion have taken on different names: intertextuality, innerbiblical exegesis (*innerbiblische Schriftauslegung*), and allusion are some of the most com-

---

90. Ibid., 1–2 (emphasis added).

91. Schmitt, Review of *Genesis und Exodus*, 457.

92. Ibid.

mon nomenclature for this phenomenon.[93] Synchronic studies must also deal with how similar texts are in relationship to one another. For the purpose of this work, these proposals will be called innerbiblical exegesis and allusion.

Studies of innerbiblical exegesis and allusion compose a growing segment in Old Testament studies. Konrad Schmid opens his article "Innerbiblische Schriftauslegung. Aspekte der Forschungsgeschichte" by saying, "Currently, the theme of innerbiblical exegesis is in great demand within Old Testament studies."[94] Of special importance for Schmid is the crisis in pentateuchal studies that led to the growing demand for innerbiblical exegesis. The "rejection of the different theories concerning the Documentary Hypothesis" corresponded to the increase in studies of innerbiblical exegesis and allusion in the Prophets.[95]

Schmid assesses the research in every corpus in the Old Testament. He suggests that the latest research in each corpus relates to the idea of innerbiblical exegesis. Innerbiblical exegesis is the reception or study of the biblical texts and subsequent comment on them. This aspect of commentary on biblical texts by biblical texts creates a relationship between the two texts. Schmid points out several new factors that have influenced biblical studies in this direction. The first factor involves a "literary-critical reading which places a methodological emphasis on redaction as innerbiblical reception."[96] Prior to this new emphasis, redaction was understood as a simple bridging of the four independent sources. Little or no interpretation was involved; the texts were conflated. As has been stated above, scholars were interested in the pristine sources written by the great authors of old. The secondary additions, however, were from epigones. Consequently, it was the pristine sources that were pursued for their theological and historical value.[97]

This elevated opinion of "secondary" remarks is another new factor. Schmid indicates that the second factor is, "the discernment of the important role of "secondary" pieces in the Old Testament. That is, there is the elimination of the theological discrediting of the supplementer as

93. For a treatment of these and various other related phenomena see Sommer, *Prophet Reads Scripture*, 1–39.

94. Schmid, "Innerbiblische Schriftauslegung," 1.

95. Ibid., 9.

96. Ibid., 3.

97. Ibid., 4–7.

a mere epigone which was resolved *a priori* in a classical manner."[98] The recognition of an interpretive process in the formation of the biblical text, most notably by Fishbane, created an awareness of biblical authors as interpreters of that material handed down.[99] This conception of the biblical author's receiving authoritative texts and making interpretive comments upon them, rather than an authorial process *ex nihilo*, gained acceptance. Those responsible for the text received the texts or traditions, interpreted them, and then passed them along in a new form. This new insight subsequently led to the new perception mentioned above concerning the compositionally connected texts. Once this process was recognized, the theological value of the final shape was reassessed and recognized as important.

THE GOALS AND LIMITS OF THE STUDY

These two factors that resulted in the increase in innerbiblical exegesis— 1) the understanding that this combination of textual units was conceived as more than mere compilation; and 2) the importance placed on the interpretive comments in this process of the combination of textual units— are particularly germane to this analysis. These two factors are important because of the relationship created between texts when two or more texts are intentionally connected with one another. A scribe or sage reads a text and comments upon the significance of that text.[100] This creative process results in a new unity, which has meaning, in part, because of the relationships between the two texts. The activity occurred within an exegetical process. It did not arrive from a mere compilation or editing of sources. Furthermore, the remarks should not be understood as insignificant. They have historical and theological value.

While these two factors and the subsequent increase in innerbiblical exegesis are significant steps in the direction of this project, they do not fully express the purpose in this work. Innerbiblical exegesis largely concerns redactional activity.[101] Redactional activity involves modifications

98. Ibid.

99. Fishbane, *Biblical Interpretation*.

100. As for whether it is a scribe or sage, see Van Seters, "Redactor in Biblical Studies," 12–16.

101. Schmid, "Innerbiblische Schriftauslegung," 3–4. For the nondistinction between redaction and composition, see Kratz, "Redaktionsgeschichte-Redaktionskritik," 367–68; Becker, *Exegese des Alten Testaments*, 87. For the distinction between redaction and

in vocalization or consonants by a later hand than the author, a rearrangement of the text, an omission, a gloss, or a redactional bridge.[102] Redaction criticism is largely concerned with the detection of the development and layers of a text.

Composition, on the other hand, involves the selection, arrangement, and adaptation of written sources in order to combine them into a meaningful whole.[103] According to Sailhamer, composition criticism "attempts to trace the ways the biblical writers organized and fashioned literary units into unified texts and whole books as well as to understand the theological characteristics of their finished works."[104] Composition involves an entire document. It begins with pieces of texts and ends with a unity.

The two golden-calf texts of Exod 32:7–20 and Deut 9:12–21 will be examined in chapter 2. This chapter will demonstrate an analysis of the relationship between the texts. Upon confirmation that an intentional relationship exists between the two texts, chapter 3 will establish a compositional strategy of innertextuality at work in light of other related passages within the Pentateuch. Innertextuality is best demonstrated when numerous connected passages are distributed throughout an entire text; if the related passages are not distributed throughout the whole, it approximates a redactional layer.[105] When proven, the compositional activity substantiates the theological intentions imprinted in the text.[106]

This analysis is concerned with the theological intentions expressed in the current shape of the Pentateuch. The current shape assumes the use of textual criticism in order to discern the appropriate text. Moreover, this analysis is not concerned with the name or personality of the author or redactor but rather with a description of meaning produced through the theological intentions.

This examination is not primarily concerned with the development of the text from one era to another; nor is it concerned with redactional layers or the theology indicated in those layers. Moreover, it is concerned

composition, see Fohrer, *Exegese des Alten Testaments*, 139–47; Van Seters, "Redactor in Biblical Studies," 1–12; Van Seters, "Ironic Circle," 487–99.

102. Fohrer, *Exegese des Alten Testaments*, 143–45.

103. Ibid., 145–47.

104. Sailhamer, *Introduction to Old Testament Theology*, 206.

105. Fohrer, *Exegese des Alten Testaments*, 143–45.

106. See chapter 2 below.

with any possibly preexistent units only insofar as those sources aid in understanding the final shape of the text.

THE IMPORTANCE OF THE TOPIC

The issue of how texts are set in relationship to one another has recently received increased attention.[107] Following the lead of that development, this work examines the relationship between Exod 32:7–20; Deut 9:12–21; Deut 32:16–21; Lev 17:1–7; Num 25:1–3; Deut 4:12–25; and Deut 31:16–31. First, this analysis will provide linguistic verification of the unity of the Pentateuch. It will accomplish this by tracing intentional, linguistic connections between these narratives, which betray a unity of purpose. Otto Eissfeldt proposed a similar notion in an article titled, "Die kleinste literarische Einheit in den Erzählungsbüchern des Alten Testaments."[108] At that time, the discipline of Old Testament research threatened to view individual narratives as disconnected from the larger whole into which they were woven. Eissfeldt demonstrated the unity of the whole by considering the links between such individual narratives.[109]

For Eissfeldt, these links showed that the distinct narratives were composed with one another in mind. Even though the content of each narrative might be different, their arrangement into an organized whole created the overall unity. It was not only the narratives of Genesis or Exodus that corroborated his thesis. The poetry of Genesis 49 and Deuteronomy 33 connected the units into a whole. These passages also had repercussions for how one should understand the narratives linked to them.[110] In a similar way, through intentional connections between the golden-calf texts, the innertextuality that this analysis demonstrates will considerably substantiate the unity of the Pentateuch.

Second, this work will contribute to the larger area of hermeneutics. It will do so because it will deal with the interrelationship of one text to another. As stated previously, the topic of innerbiblical exegesis and allusion within biblical studies has generated a great deal of interest. In his article "Innerbiblische Schriftauslegung," Schmid first appraises the development of Old Testament scholarship that led to the growth of

---

107. Schmid, "Innerbiblische Schriftauslegung."
108. Eissfeldt, "Kleinste Literarische Einheit," 143–49.
109. Ibid., 149.
110. Ibid., 146.

innerbiblical exegesis and allusion. While reviewing the current research in this area, he writes, "A true boom of publications within the topic [*innerbiblische Schriftauslegung*] began at the close of the 1970's and currently continues and, in fact, is still growing."[111] Schmid's article illustrates the growing interest in innerbiblical exegesis and allusion.

Innerbiblical exegesis, synchronic studies of the Old Testament, diachronic studies of the Old Testament, methodology that ascertains a connection between texts, and the New Testament's use of the Old are all areas in which these issues of textual relationships are being examined.[112] Furthermore, these studies both reveal and contribute to the discussion of how texts relate to one another in the larger field of literary theory.

Third, this analysis will contribute to the area of pentateuchal studies. It will accomplish this 1) by observing exegetical details of the passages involved, making an analysis of their relationship, and showing the results of the comparison; 2) by mapping the compositional strategies within the present shape of the Pentateuch; and 3) by contributing to the contemporary expression of the theology of the Pentateuch.

Fourth, in conjunction with textually related studies, this work will open avenues of relationship between these and related biblical texts. So it will provide an understanding of how these texts were received by authors of subsequent texts. This includes New Testament passages such as 1 Cor 10:1–22.

---

111. Schmid, "Innerbiblische Schriftauslegung," 11.

112. Ibid. For synchronic- and diachronic-related issues, see Sommer, "Exegesis, Allusion and Intertextuality in the Hebrew Bible." For one example of methodology concerning the allusion of a New Testament author to the Old Testament, see Hays, *Echoes of Scripture*, 25–33.

1

Innertextuality and Biblical Authorship

A CENTRAL CONCERN FOR Old Testament theology is an understanding of the final shape of the canon.[1] Thus, a central concern for the basis of this project is an understanding of the final shape of the Pentateuch. In his *The Canonical Hebrew Bible: A Theology of the Old Testament*, Rolf Rendtorff describes his task as "allowing the intentions of those who gave the texts their present shape to come into their own ... The guiding interest is not the uncovering of tensions or contradictions in the texts, however, but rather the question how the authors of the extant texts understood them in their present form and how they wanted their readers to understand them."[2] The task as Rendtorff saw it was to explain the text in its present shape by discerning the intentions of those who shaped it.

Rendtorff is balancing two opposing poles in order to focus on this task. The first pole concerns the issues dealt with in the introduction to this work. The task of literary criticism was an attempt to isolate the different sources within a text in order to explain those sources. This process resulted in a loss of concern for the final shape of the text.

The other pole attempts to gloss over the "tensions or contradictions in the texts."[3] This pole treats the text in a harmonizing manner. It attempts to smooth out the complexities of the final shape in order to arrive at a uniform reading. In doing so, this pole also fails to take seriously the final shape of the text. Rendtorff avoided these poles in an attempt to understand the final shape. Rendtorff maintains "that each biblical text in the form in which we now have it has its own statement to make."[4]

---

1. See the introduction of this work as well as Rendtorff, *Canonical Hebrew Bible*, 1–2, 719; Sailhamer, "Biblical Theology and the Composition of the Hebrew Bible," 25–37.

2. Rendtorff, *Canonical Hebrew Bible*, 3.

3. Ibid.

4. Ibid., 720.

For Rendtorff, this statement of the text can be comprehended neither by dividing the text nor by glossing over any apparent complexities.

The complexities are observable data that have often been used to delineate sources. A complexity might be a repeated storyline, phrase, or term, the absence of smooth or typical syntax, or the use of alternate names. These complexities exist in the final shape of the text, however, and can be used to discern the intentions imprinted in that shape. These complexities often reveal the process of selection, arrangement, adaptation, and writing of smaller units of texts in order to create a larger whole in a structured and meaningful manner. The task of biblical studies should be to explain the text, along with any complexities in order to arrive at the message of the final shape.

This analysis also seeks to balance these opposing poles. Its aim is not an isolation of the sources that make up the Pentateuch. Neither is its aim primarily an attempt to understand the historical development of how the current Pentateuch came into being. Moreover, it is not at attempt at harmonization. The narratives of Exod 32:7–20 and Deut 9:12–21 do contain certain complexities. An attempt will not be made to level the surface of these two narratives and harmonize the differences between them. Rather, this work asks, why does the final shape of the Pentateuch contain these two narratives? As Rendtorff said concerning his attempt to understand the final shape, "it is a matter of changing the set of questions to be asked and the exegetical interest."[5] The interest of this analysis lies in the final shape of the Pentateuch and the intentions embodied in it.

This chapter will provide an interpretive basis for discerning these intentions. The first section will define the term *innertextuality* and interact with others who have demonstrated similar notions from biblical passages. The second section will relate innertextuality to the authorship of biblical books.

INNERTEXTUALITY

This section will introduce the notion of innertextuality and give its definition. Each integral part of the definition will be discussed in the following subsections. The term, innertextuality, is understood as an intentional connection between texts in order to combine them into a larger whole. These connections are used to produce a structure through which an

---

5. Ibid., 719.

author communicates a message. John Sailhamer, in his *Introduction to Old Testament Theology: A Canonical Approach*, discusses this phenomenon. Sailhamer views innertextuality as a strategy of authorial composition. Such strategies of composition "make up the whole fabric of biblical narrative books. Such inner-linkage binding narratives into a larger whole is called inner-textuality. By means of such links the biblical authors thematize their basic message."[6] What Sailhamer calls "inner-linkage" and "links" are the linguistic connections between different textual units. These connections between narratives serve to join the narratives together. If the connections are distributed throughout an entire unit, a composition is constructed by means of the connections.

These connections reveal the strategies and intentions imprinted in the text. A reader pursues understanding by detecting the strategies "embodied in the text."[7] This work assumes that a biblical book is a reflection of an author's, that is, a composer's intention.[8] The name or personality of the author is not the objective for the current purposes. Rather, the current shape, the content of the text and the strategies contained therein contribute to the message communicated through the text. The following section will discuss the first integral component of innertextuality, the connection between textual units.

Connections between Texts

This section will discuss the first aspect of innertextuality, the connection between textual units. These connections between textual units are a primary feature of innertextuality. They are more than random links that a reader associates between texts. They are formal characteristics constituting texts. A connection consists of formal linguistic elements that exist in two or more passages. Terminological, syntactical, and stylistic characteristics are able to signal the connections between textual units, which indicate signs of compositional activity. The final section of this chapter will lay the methodological groundwork for determining the intentionality of these connections. Once demonstrated, an intentional connection

---

6. Sailhamer, *Old Testament Theology*, 209.

7. Ibid., 202, 204. For a fuller description of intentionality and its relationship to this work, see the following section concerning biblical authorship.

8. On the distinction between author and redactor see note 9 in the introduction and the following section concerning biblical authorship.

exhibits the design of an author and leaves an imprint reflected through linguistic signs.

Sailhamer illustrates an example of this intentional connection at key positions within the Pentateuch. He explains,

> At three macro-structural junctures in the Pentateuch, the author has spliced a major poetic discourse onto the end of a large unit of narrative (Ge 49; Nu 24; Dt 31). A close look at the material lying between and connecting the narrative and poetic sections reveals the presence of a homogeneous compositional stratum. It is most noticeably marked by the recurrence of the same terminology and narrative motifs. In each of the three segments (especially Ge 49:1; Nu 24:14; Dt 31:28–29), the central narrative figure (Jacob, Balaam, Moses) calls an audience together (imperative) and proclaims (cohortative) what will happen in the "end of days."[9]

In detecting the repetition of expressions and subject matter Sailhamer has uncovered traces of compositional activity. Sailhamer explains the expressions and subject matter of each passage and concludes: "Such convergence of macro-structure, narrative motifs, and terminology among these three strategically important poems of the Pentateuch can hardly be accidental. The fact that the terms occur only one other time in the Pentateuch, and that also within a macro-structural seam (Deut 4), argues strongly for our taking these connecting segments to be the work of the final composer or author of the Pentateuch."[10] Sailhamer detects formal qualities such as terminology and narrative motifs through which these passages are connected. The similarities connect the passages to one another and give the Pentateuch a shape or structure.

The poems used at these junctures also betray an intentional connection. Sailhamer points out an agreement of phraseology between Gen 49:9 and Num 24:9. He states, "Such verbatim use of one text by another through quotation and allusion is the means by which themes and theological ideas are carried along and developed within the compositional strategy of the book."[11] The final shape exhibits an association between these poems. The virtually exact phraseology suggests that this is not coincidental but instead purposeful. The linguistic connections expressed through the verbatim use of a textual unit by two or more passages expose

9. Sailhamer, *Introduction to Old Testament Theology*, 210–11.

10. Ibid.

11. Ibid., 211–12.

the theological intentions in the composition. The following sections will give examples of connections between textual units from four scholars' conception of them.

GEORG FOHRER

An intentional connection between narratives coheres with the notion of composition. This section will discuss the notion of a connection between textual units in light of Georg Fohrer's definition of composition. In his book *Exegese des Alten Testaments: Einführung in Die Methodik*, Georg Fohrer discusses characteristics of redaction and characteristics of a composition. A key characteristic of a composition is the inclusion of a unit into a "complex of several units which are meaningfully and purposefully joined together."[12] Fohrer maintains that a composition is several units fitted together into a larger, structured whole. Fohrer's understanding is that the units must *fit with* one another.

How does Fohrer perceive this notion of fitting together? He sees it when the individual units point to a greater context.[13] Fohrer mentions different possibilities that point to a greater context. One possibility, in particular, is important for the purposes here. He says, "More important are structural similarities between several collections in which compositions are assumed and with which the same construction can arise . . . Also formal and linguistic characteristics which are consistently repeated in the units forming a composition can also play a role. A structural comparison of the units can lead to those units which perhaps belong to a composition. The meaningful and purposeful framework is decisive."[14] Fohrer argues that formal and linguistic elements of a textual unit which consistently recur point to a composition.

These reappearing formal and linguistic elements connect individual units into a larger whole. For Fohrer, this connectivity between units and throughout the whole assists in distinguishing composition from redaction. These reappearing characteristics, which are formal and linguistic in manner, are consistent with the connection between texts within innertextuality.

---

12. Fohrer, *Exegese des Alten Testaments*, 145.
13. Ibid.
14. Ibid.

MARKUS WITTE

This section will discuss the notion of a connection between textual units in light of Markus Witte's examination of Genesis 1–11. In his book *Die Biblische Urgeschichte: Redaktions- und Theologiegeschichtliche Beobachtungen zu Genesis 1:1—11:26*, Witte considers these connections woven into the fabric of different textual units. Witte examines the final shape of Genesis 1–11 and attempts to identify the redactional bridges that serve to unite the primeval history.[15]

Witte maintains that the profile of the final redaction of the primeval history can be identified by isolating and examining certain redactional bridges in the primeval history.[16] After these basic entries are examined (Gen 2:4; 4:25–26; 6:1–4), one can proceed to other passages that are "directly associated with the redactional bridges in form, content, and terminology."[17] Witte discerns the composition of the final shape of the primeval history by identifying passages connected in the overall unit. Characteristics formal, terminological, and content related connect the passages.

Witte eventually finds that Gen 2:4; 4:25–26; 6:1–4, et al. serve four important purposes for the primeval history. First, these passages "have the same redactional intention ... and leave an imprint of the compositional profile of the primeval history."[18] Second, these passages exhibit a technique that combines the two larger units by means of terminology. This produces a syntactical unit.[19] Third, this technique also involves special conceptions (*Begriffe*) and motifs, which provide a transition between the larger units.[20] Finally, these passages also make available "characteristic notions, motifs, sentence constructions, and theological perceptions."[21]

---

15. Witte, *Die Biblische Urgeschichte*, 78.

16. Ibid., 45–53, 77–78.

17. Ibid., 51. It is not my purpose here to draw a distinction between redaction and composition. The similarity in methodology is instructive at this point. The fact that Witte's focus is on Genesis 1–11 and not the entirety of the Pentateuch is a sufficient reason for using his methodology and yet still acknowledging a distinction between redaction and composition.

18. Ibid., 77.

19. Ibid., 78.

20. Ibid.

21. Ibid.

These passages subsequently provide an important framework from which to discern the remaining connections within the primeval history.

Witte's methodology relates to the notion of innertextuality. It does so in relation to formal, terminological, and content-related connections that link the texts together. Witte draws out the formal characteristics that provide the basis for the connections. These connections then give a foundation from which to interpret the strategies to which they point. This aspect of Witte's methodology is congruent with the notion of connections between textual units in innertextuality.

ROLF RENDTORFF

This section will discuss the notion of a connection between textual units in light of Rolf Rendtorff's examination of formulaic speech. An intentional connection can be understood from the perspective of formulaic speech. Formulaic speech is a characteristic expression originally used in a particular *Sitz im Leben*.[22] An expression can be used, however, in various contexts of biblical texts. In his book *The Canonical Hebrew Bible: A Theology of the Old Testament*, Rendtorff's interest is not in the *Sitz im Leben* of a particular formulaic expression but rather in its usage and purpose within the biblical books and canon.[23] Understood from this perspective, formulaic speech takes into account a similar phenomenon as the connections between texts in innertextuality. Rendtorff comments that "particular linguistic elements are frequently found in quite different contexts."[24] The "particular linguistic elements" comprise similar terminology or phraseology. These formulaic elements are used in various contexts within biblical books or the canon. The interplay of these elements connects the various passages.

In a discussion involving the "I-Am" formula, Rendtorff demonstrates the importance of the connections within the Pentateuch. In Exod 6:2–8, this characteristic formula is used a number of times. Rendtorff notes how the element in this passage connects it to others. He states, "Here the section of the story that is beginning, so fundamental for Israel's identity, is linked backwards with the story of the forefathers and forwards with the gift of the promised land. This is expressed in a unique

---

22. Rendtorff, *Canonical Hebrew Bible*, 726.

23. Ibid., 726–34.

24. Ibid., 726.

linking and interweaving of different characteristic form elements."[25] For Rendtorff also, these similar expressions substantiate a connection between passages. This corresponds to the notion of connections between textual units in innertextuality defined in this chapter.

Otto Eissfeldt

This section will discuss the notion of a connection between textual units in light of Otto Eissfeldt's examination of the smallest literary unit. Otto Eissfeldt recognized the importance of these internal connections between textual units in his essay "Die kleinste literarische Einheit in den Erzählungsbüchern des Alten Testaments."[26] At the time, studies in the Old Testament threatened to view individual narratives as disconnected from the larger source into which they were woven. In the essay, Eissfeldt noted how different passages within a source were written with one another in mind. These connections between passages demonstrated Eissfeldt's thesis about the relationship of smaller units of narrative within the whole: Individual narratives had a distinct subject matter but their present shape did not exist outside of their current biblical context.

Eissfeldt was attempting to show the cohesion of the individual narratives within their particular source. He first had to establish comparable elements between the individual narratives. Similar terminology, corresponding narrative sequence, and parallel motifs connected the units to one another.[27] He illustrates: "It is understood that the creation story of (P) is told with the flood history and that one has the other as a necessary prerequisite. Genesis 1:31, 'And God saw everything which he had made and saw that it was very good' and 6:12, 'And God saw the earth and saw that it was spoiled' are from the outset drafted in view of one another."[28] Eissfeldt relates the passages to one another because of analogous terms, narrative sequence, and parallel motifs. From his perspective, the narratives are intentionally written in light of one another. This can be understood, Eissfeldt argues, because of similar elements found in both passages. This association of passages because of analogous elements is

---

25. Ibid., 727.

26. Eissfeldt, "Die kleinste literarische Einheit," 143–49.

27. Ibid., 144–48.

28. Ibid., 144.

consistent with the notion of connection between textual units within innertextuality.

Texts are associated with one another when similar formal elements exist. These elements show a relationship between the texts. The issue of recurring formal elements and related phenomena will resurface in the final section of this chapter dealing with methodology. At that point, the consideration will be whether or not these formal elements substantiate an intentional connection. If such intentionality can be substantiated, what does it indicate about its inclusion into a larger whole? These connections also have implications for the boundary of a text.

This section has attempted to demonstrate the notion of formal linguistic connections between texts from four scholars' understanding of how textual units are connected together into a larger literary context. The following section will discuss how the connections between texts have implications for the boundaries of a larger unit. It will do so by showing scholars' use of these connections in determining the boundary of a unit.

The Combination of a Smaller Textual Unit into a Larger Whole

This section will show how the connections between texts point to the combination of smaller textual units into a larger whole. Scholars have long recognized the importance the boundaries of a text have for understanding of a text.[29] These connections of textual units in innertextuality show the boundaries of a larger unit and thus have implications for discerning a larger unified text.

OTTO EISSFELDT

Eissfeldt's article demonstrated that the boundaries of whole textual units were not the individual narratives that make up a book like Genesis. Instead the boundary of an entire textual unit could be discerned through the combination of individual narratives into an entirety, that is, into a larger whole.[30] Literary criticism had observed the complexities within the pentateuchal narratives. The discernment of an ever-increasing number of complexities were threatening to destroy the recognition of the unity of each of the four main sources of J, E, D, and P. Scholars were focusing on

29. Muilenburg, "Form Criticism and Beyond," 8–10.
30. Eissfeldt, "Die kleinste literarische Einheit," 144–48.

isolated layers or independent units within a source. Eissfeldt, however, recognized a disintegration of the different sources and expressed a concern. In his reading of the Pentateuch, he noticed that the narratives and poems were connected in various ways. Although the subject matter was different, the narratives were written with one another in mind.[31]

Because of this, the boundary of the unit extended beyond the individual narratives. Eissfeldt states, "The limits of an independent unit of narrative are to be placed as far as needed for the horizon of the particular narrative. If this goes beyond an 'individual narrative' and its elements of interrelated components which are pointing backwards and forwards from it, then it is no independent literary unit, but a part of a larger whole."[32] Eissfeldt recognizes the importance that these interrelated elements have for the boundary of a textual unit. They force the interpreter to consider the individual narratives in light of the larger whole unit. The related components of the individual narratives point backward and forwards and give the larger whole, which the related components indicate, a sense of coherence and boundary.

After reviewing the examples of connections between pentateuchal narratives, Eissfeldt concludes, "As a result, the links here are the components which constitute the narratives, not just secondary additions."[33] These similar elements that make up the links between narrative accounts are not mere bridges between narratives. Instead they actually make up the larger whole. Eissfeldt was concerned with demonstrating the unity of the Priestly Source. He continues with the same concern for the Elohist and the Yahwist. His observation, however, is applicable to the entire Pentateuch.[34] The boundaries of a literary unit extend to the border of these formally connected texts. These connections between textual units demonstrate the combination of smaller textual units into a larger whole.

---

31. Ibid., 143.

32. Ibid., 144.

33. Ibid., 145.

34. The application of Eissfeldt's thesis to the entire Pentateuch was made known to me in a conversation with my major professor, John Sailhamer, at Southeastern Baptist Theological Seminary in the spring semester of 2004.

RENDTORFF

This section will show how Rendtorff uses the notion of formulaic speech to connect smaller units into a larger whole. It will also point out other scholars' use of a combination of smaller units to point to the boundaries of a larger unit. Rendtorff asserts the significance of recurring, formal connections for textual boundaries. He discusses the I-Am formula within the Pentateuch and comments on its occurrence in Exod 6:2–8. He says, "Here the section of the story that is beginning, so fundamental for Israel's identity, is linked backwards with the story of the forefathers and forwards with the gift of the promised land."[35] It is this formulaic expression that links the individual narratives together. Rendtorff considers two types of formulaic speech. One type is woven throughout the Pentateuch while the second type is limited to a narrow context. That type of formulaic speech distributed throughout the whole most closely relates to the notion of innertextuality.

Innertextuality is a strategy by which individual units of text are combined into a larger whole. This is accomplished by a distribution of recurring formal characteristics throughout the entirety of a work. Formal connections that relate to an immediate context, to a smaller section of a book, or to a random connection between passages likely fall short of innertextuality. When limited to an immediate passage these types of connections are called in-textuality.[36] Fohrer also discusses these connections which are not distributed throughout an entire work and categorizes them as redaction.[37] Moreover, in his discussion of formulaic speech, Rendtorff mentions formulaic expressions that "remain limited to their immediate area of validity."[38] Because these similar expressions "are not used outside their own area of application," they are not the same type of formulaic connection that Rendtorff expresses earlier, which is woven throughout the Pentateuch.[39] In this way Rendtorff's notion of formulaic speech encompasses a similar phenomenon to linguistic connections between textual units. When these connections are used in individual passages and distributed throughout, they point to a larger whole.

35. Rendtorff, *The Canonical Hebrew Bible*, 727.
36. Sailhamer, *Old Testament Theology*, 207–9.
37. Fohrer, *Exegese des Alten Testaments*, 143–47.
38. Rendtorff, *The Canonical Hebrew Bible*, 734.
39. Ibid.

The effect that innertextuality exerts on the unity of a book should not be overlooked. Fohrer takes into account these formal connections between units when considering a composition. The formal connections point to a greater context beyond the boundaries of an individual narrative.[40] Likewise, Witte emphasizes the effect that the formal connections have on the unity of a text. He contends that the formal characteristics existing between Gen 2:4; 4:25–26; 6:1–4; 6:7aβ, 7aγ, 7b; 7:1b, 3, 8–9, 23aα, and 23aβ "in each case combine separately existing conceptions and motifs of the 'priestly' and 'yahwistic' layer into a syntactical unit."[41] These remarks reveal the way in which similar formal elements between two or more accounts are able to unite those accounts into a single work.

Innertextuality can bring the unity of the work into view. Rendtorff expresses a similar sentiment as he examines the covenant formula. He concludes, "Thus the covenant formula encompasses "priestly" as well as Deuteronomic texts in the present final form of the Pentateuch."[42] Rendtorff notes here that the similar turns of expression that comprise formulaic conceptions span across priestly and Deuteronomic texts. The use of innertextuality recognizes the composition of smaller units into a larger whole. In saying this, however, its use also acknowledges the importance of these smaller units for discerning the theological intentions imprinted in the entire unit. These factors led him to the conclusion that the present shape of the Pentateuch represents an intended unity with a theological message. This section has shown the importance of the linguistic connections in discerning the boundaries of a unit. The next section shows the implication of the linguistic connections for discerning theological intentions.

Discerning Theological Intentions

The definition of *innertextuality* found earlier in this chapter stated that the linkages between narratives produce a structure through which an author communicates a message. A later section will deal more fully with discerning intentionality as it relates to authorship and composition. In this section, however, a discussion of several scholars' work will demonstrate how the formal, linguistic connections between passages show

40. Fohrer, *Exegese des Alten Testaments*, 145.

41. Witte, *Die Biblische Urgeschichte*, 78.

42. Rendtorff, *Canonical Hebrew Bible*, 731.

intentionality and create a semantic effect. The repeated connections comprising innertextuality reveal intentionality at work. They extend beyond coincidence to expose intentional connections and structuring.

In his discussion of innertextuality, Sailhamer notes its significance when discerning theological intentions. He states, "Such inner-linkage binding narratives into a larger whole is called inner-textuality. By means of such links the biblical authors thematize their basic message."[43] Sailhamer continues with a demonstration of the innertextuality within the compositional seams of the Pentateuch. He concludes his discussion by stating that "such verbatim use of one text by another through quotation and allusion is the means by which themes and theological ideas are carried along and developed within the compositional strategy of the book."[44] These connections call attention to the message verbalized in the text and direct the reader toward the purpose of communication.

Rendtorff also discusses the significance of recurring expressions in relation to meaning. In a discussion of a particular formulaic expression, Rendtorff explains that this expression "shows what the linguistic options are for expressing primarily theological matters and connections in the flexible use of formulaic elements; and it shows how these are perceived by the authors of Hebrew Bible texts."[45] Authors used the formulaic expressions to advance their message through those expressions available to them. It was through these formulaic texts that authors produced the intended effect. In a discussion of the grace formula, Rendtorff concludes, "In its various forms, the grace formula thus puts God's qualities into words in an exemplary manner and shows itself thus to be an important element of the linguistic shaping of the theological insights and experiences of the biblical authors."[46] These formulas, which consist of recurring terminological, syntactical, and stylistic expressions, become a key component of the way in which biblical authors express themselves.

Another formulaic expression plays a particularly important role within the Pentateuch. Rendtorff explains, "Here we shall draw attention once again to the predominant synchronic function of the [covenant] formula. In the structure of the Pentateuch as a whole the covenant formula

---

43. Sailhamer, *Old Testament Theology*, 209–10.
44. Ibid., 211–12.
45. Rendtorff, *Canonical Hebrew Bible*, 733.
46. Ibid., 734.

has an important function. It stands at the beginning in connection with Abraham in Gen. 17.7 and at the end in Deut 29.12. In both texts the covenant formula appears as the direct explanation of the 'covenant' (*b*ᵉ*rit*); this close connection is found only in these two passages in the Hebrew Bible, which can scarcely be regarded as a coincidence."[47] Rendtorff demonstrates the connection between these important passages related to the covenant formula. Such a relationship is beyond coincidence and consequently reveals the purpose for the connection.

Terminological, syntactical, and stylistic connections within a book directly pertain to understanding a text in an appropriate context. Christopher Seitz illustrates this matter in his article concerning the Twelve: "On Letting a Text 'Act Like a Man'—the Book of the Twelve: New Horizons for Canonical Reading, with Hermeneutical Reflections."[48] Seitz reviews terminological and phrasal connections between the individual prophetic books in order to work out questions of canonical arrangement. Seitz draws an implication from this canonical arrangement of the Twelve and adds to this by noting "observations about beginnings and endings of books; repeated themes, like the compassionate-formula, or drought and famine and their opposites; or reader-oriented appeals to learn from the past and re-orient oneself towards God's ways and self, it becomes clear that the placement of later books next to earlier ones is an intentional move, arising from the canonical process itself . . ."[49] It is these correspondences in terminology and theme between the beginnings and endings of individual prophetic books and repeated formulas that give the Twelve a canonical shape. Seitz shows how these factors bring one to the conclusion that the arrangement of the Twelve, and therefore a legitimate manner in which to interpret it, is inherent in the canonical process. It is the recurring formulas and similar terminology that exhibit the canonical process.

Shimon Bar-Efrat also draws attention to the importance of structural connections within a textual unit for discerning meaning.[50] Bar-Efrat is primarily concerned with the structural analysis of narratives, but his

---

47. Ibid., 731.

48. Seitz, "On Letting a Text 'Act Like a Man.'"

49. Ibid., 165.

50. Bar-Efrat, "Some Observations on the Analysis of Structure."

observations relate to entire books or a larger unit.[51] Bar-Efrat discerns intentionality through the inner-relationships within the narrative. He maintains that inner-relationships affect an appropriate understanding of a textual unit.[52]

Bar-Efrat analyzes different elements upon which to base a structural analysis. The first level relates closely with the notion of innertextuality dealing with the repetition of terminology. Bar-Efrat explains,

> The analysis of structure on this level is based on words or phrases. For example, the creation account in the first chapter of Genesis has a very distinct structure, which even the most superficial reader cannot fail to notice. This structure, which divides the whole account into seven well-defined sections, is clearly marked by the recurrent phrase: "And it was evening and it was morning, the *n*th day." In addition we find repetition of phrases such as: "And God said, Let …" "and God saw that it was good" which also contributes to the manifestation of the structure.[53]

Bar-Efrat bases the analysis of the narrative on repetition within the narrative. The repeated elements connect certain portions of the text and provide the framework of the narrative.

This framework or structure gives a basis for interpretation. In his closing section, Bar-Efrat relates the notion of structure to meaning. He concludes, "Structure has rhetorical and expressive value: it is one of the factors governing the effect of the work on the reader and in addition it serves to express or accentuate meaning."[54] When used within a larger whole, the inner-relationships of connected elements also provide a basis for interpretation. While repeated formal characteristics distributed throughout an entire book do not imitate a symmetrical frame such as Genesis 1, nevertheless, repeated phrases approximating innertextuality provide some structure that influences interpretation. One has only to think of the *toledot* formulas in Genesis, or the "day of the Lord" motif of the book of the Twelve for examples.[55] Innertextuality by definition connects distinct units. These distinct units also contribute to the overall effect of the whole. Without the innertextuality, however, there

51. Ibid., 155–57.

52. Ibid., 172.

53. Ibid., 157.

54. Ibid., 172.

55. Rendtorff, "How to Read the Book of the Twelve as a Theological Unity," 75–87.

would be little on which to base an interpretation of the juxtaposition of individual units.

To summarize the notion of innertextuality, recurring formal connections bring a sense of unity to a text and provide the structure or framework to a unit. Consequently, they provide a formal basis for interpretation. Additionally, particular repeated texts also have a sense of commentary. Often it is those texts that occur at the end of a book or at a key juncture that exert such influence. Eissfeldt notes such a case in the blessings and curses of Genesis 49 and Deut 33:7. He writes, "Furthermore, the seemingly entirely isolated narratives of Reuben's disgraceful deed with Bilha (Gen 35:21, 22), Simeon and Levi's wickedness to Shechem (Gen 34), Judah and Tamar (Gen 38), and the curses concerning Reuben, Simeon, and Levi (Gen 49:1–7) which have repercussions on these narratives, as well the blessings for Judah in Deut 33:7 which apply to the passage concerning Judah (Gen 49:8–12) show . . . that they are only understandable as part of a larger whole."[56] Eissfeldt's main point demonstrates that the connections between the textual units form a larger whole. Eissfeldt also indicates that the poetry of Genesis 49 has an effect on the earlier narratives. He correctly appreciates how the allusions that occur in the poetic seams of Genesis 49 and Deuteronomy 33 fold back upon and interpret the prior narratives.[57] These connections between different narratives and between narrative and poetry provide an interpretive framework for the book.

Innertextuality thus involves different units of text associated with one another through formal linguistic elements. This section has shown how these formal elements connect the textual unit into a larger whole and provide a basis for discerning the theological intentions. The question naturally arises about the way in which these units of text were combined into a larger whole. What was the method of composition? How did the Pentateuch in its approximate shape come into being? These questions relate to the notion of biblical authorship. The following section will relate this view of innertextuality to the notion of biblical authorship.

---

56. Eissfeldt, "Die kleinste literarische Einheit," 146.

57. For a related notion, see Sailhamer, *Introduction to Old Testament Theology*, 210–12; and Sailhamer, *Pentateuch as Narrative*, 233–38, 408–9, 477–78.

INNERTEXTUALITY AND BIBLICAL AUTHORSHIP

This section will propose a particular understanding of how biblical texts are combined into a whole. It will do so by discussing three text-formation models. Moreover, this chapter will define the composition of biblical books and show how innertextuality coheres within the composition of those texts. Innertextuality involves an intentional connection between texts. What texts are involved? Did the texts exist in another document or independently? How did they arrive at the locale in which they reside? This book seeks to examine these questions in light of passages within the Pentateuch that relate to the idolatry of the golden calf. The two central passages dealing with the incident of the golden calf compel some interesting questions: How did the person responsible for the final shape perceive these two passages relating to one another? Did the author use one narrative upon which to form the other? Is there a common source for the two? Is the author intentionally associating the two passages to construct his overall meaning? These questions concerning authorship are important in light of the differences between the culture in which the Bible was composed and our modern technological age.

From a modern vantage point, one might assume that an author writes the way most readers read, that is, from beginning to end. Or to put it another way, an author proceeds from a beginning point and progresses through a written work by writing and creating as he or she moves toward the end. And yet is this understanding appropriate for Old Testament material? William Schniedewind raises this issue in his text *How the Bible Became a Book*. He writes, "We tend to read the Bible through the lens of modernity. This is to say, we read the Bible as a book. Not only do we tend to think of the Bible as a single book, but we also read the Bible as if it came from a world of texts, books, and authors. We read the Bible from our own perspective of a highly literate world. Yet, the Bible was written before there were books."[58] Schniedewind causes the modern-day reader to question the notion of how biblical authorship is viewed. He does this by casting doubt on the untried opinion that the Bible came from a culture not unlike the modern culture of print, writing, and books.

If the Bible was not written in a manner similar to a modern notion of authorship, then how was it written? A description of authorship from

---

58. Schniedewind, *How the Bible Became a Book*, 3.

the pages of the Bible itself is rare.[59] Did biblical authors sit down and write their full text in a single setting? Did they use preexistent material? The following section attempts to deal with these issues by examining three text-formation models and proposing a particular model that coheres with the notion of innertextuality.

Recent Text-Formation Models

A goal of contemporary Old Testament scholarship is understanding the final shape of the canon. This does not mean, however, that one should attempt to read the text in a harmonizing or absolutely smooth manner without a concern for indicators that betray the method of its production. In this case the reader would have to ignore uneven transitions, repetitions, and breaks in typical structure that arise when one reads a passage. This work will demonstrate that a biblical author has used smaller textual units in order to compose a text. The complex makeup of biblical texts is important in that it reveals the manner in which a text was composed. These features mark the form and structure of the final shape. The form and structure of the text serve as a means to communicate a message. Therefore it is important to ask how these texts formed. Different models have been proposed that in some way reflect the details found in the biblical text.

INNERBIBLICAL EXEGESIS

In *Biblical Interpretation in Ancient Israel* Michael Fishbane describes the process by which biblical texts were handed down and subsequently commented upon by those who handled them.[60] This section will discuss a model of textual formation known as innerbiblical exegesis. Fishbane's model concerns the growth of textual material through exegesis. For Fishbane, different groups of people with various motivations read the received texts and supplemented the existing text with notations. They did so for different reasons, with a resulting accumulation of textual material. This accumulation can now be detected because of characteristics that exemplify the notations that were made.

The different characteristics involve technical formulae that indicate a comment on another passage, comparing parallel texts within or between

---

59. Von Rad, *Old Testament Theology*, 40–49.

60. Fishbane, *Biblical Interpretation*.

the Masoretic tradition or a version of it and certain redundant features of texts—whether they be terms, phrases, or variants.[61] For Fishbane, the discernable features of accumulation give occasion for a particular way of understanding the individual intentions reflected in each case.

Fishbane organizes the notations of biblical text, what he calls, innerbiblical exegesis, under four categories. What is important for the purposes here, however, has to do with how Fishbane envisions these texts forming. That is, how does the text, reflected in the final shape of the canon, come into being? For Fishbane, the process has to do with glosses or interpretations, i.e., exegesis, which attempts to explain the text in question. Scribes and others have taken the authoritative text (*traditum*) and commented upon those texts (*traditio*). These glosses have resulted in the final shape of the canonical texts. This process involves how a text is received and then passed on to another generation of readers; it involves an innerbiblical exegesis.

REDACTION

This section will discuss another model of textual formation, redaction. Although redaction continues to be defined within the scholarly guild, Fohrer's definition will guide the discussion here.[62] Fohrer asserts that redaction involves the combination of individual units which are disconnected or the combination of individual units in a manner which does not link the units into a structured whole.[63] Links that combine narratives into a structured whole relate to composition.[64] For Fohrer, 1) redaction can be understood as a method for passing down otherwise independent units of tradition, or 2) redaction can be viewed as a particular imprint that has been left on an otherwise-independent unit. In these cases, redaction should not be viewed as creating a new structured and purposeful whole but rather should be viewed as leaving an indention, an impression, a layer, on an otherwise independent unit.[65]

---

61. Ibid., 42–43, 291.

62. Fohrer, *Exegese des Alten Testaments*, 119–50. For another view of redaction and composition, see Van Seters, "An Ironic Circle," 487–99. Cf. Becker, *Exegese des Alten Testaments*, 77–97. Kratz, "Redaktionsgeschichte-Redaktionskritik," 367–78; Schmid, "Innerbiblische Schriftauslegung," 1–22.

63. Fohrer, *Exegese des Alten Testaments*, 141.

64. Ibid., 139.

65. Ibid., 147.

The final shapes in any of these cases would have been produced in a redactional manner. In the former case a compilation of independent texts was produced. The independent narratives making up that compilation have no purposeful or meaningful arrangement. In the latter case, encroachments or additions to the otherwise independent unit have taken place. Texts described as independent units subsequently received imprints, that is, some type of literary impress that affected the work.

COMPOSITION

This section will deal with the third model of textual formation: composition. Fohrer also discusses composition and how it relates to textual formation. Composition exists when at least two units of text have been brought together to form a meaningful whole.[66] Composition entails a creative process that involves any aspect of authoring or composing which brings a textual work into a greater whole. Different features that recur throughout a textual work and that subsequently bring structure, purpose, and meaning to the whole work exemplify a composition. Recurring features such as superscriptions and postscripts, structural similarities, and linguistic content are all able to point to a composition. Mere redactional appendages not consistent with the larger whole are not compositional in nature. A combination of independent units without a structured or purposeful unity simply points to a redaction.[67] A composition involves features distributed throughout the textual unit and that consequently bring that work into a meaningful and purposeful structure.[68]

Composition involves a very distinct phenomenon in contrast to an innerbiblical model or a redactional model. Unlike innerbiblical exegesis or redaction, composition is not isolated to an immediate context but should be distributed throughout a textual unit. Furthermore, a composition is constructed in a manner that brings an ordered intention to the entire work. Similar to innerbiblical exegesis, however, composition does involve a reception and interpretation of texts.[69] These texts are selected, arranged, adapted and written in order to fit into a larger and purposeful whole. This section has described three text-formation models: inner-

---

66. Ibid., 139; Van Seters, "An Ironic Circle."

67. Fohrer, *Exegese des Alten Testaments*, 146.

68. Ibid., 145.

69. See below, pp. 47–53.

biblical exegesis, redaction, and composition. The following section will define composition and relate it to innertextuality.

Composition

The approach to biblical authorship in this work is compositional. This section will briefly define composition before proceeding to the notion of intentionality and meaning. Composition is the selection, arrangement, adaptation, and writing of textual units in order to create a larger whole in a structured and meaningful way.[70]

The notion of selection can be seen from various observations. First, it appears when smaller units of text are used within a larger whole. These smaller units are recognized by observing repeated storylines, phrases, or terms; the absence of smooth or typical syntax; or the use of alternate names. Often one or more of these features can be discerned along the edges of these smaller units. Thus these units appear to be selected from other locations. Examples of such selection can be discerned through observations as basic as the transition in syntax, style, and terminology between the textual unit of Gen 1:1—2:3 and the subsequent textual unit of Gen 2:5—2:25. On the other hand, they can be as complex as recognizing the uneven transitions and repetitions in the syntax and terminology in a chapter such as Exodus 19.

Second, selection appears when smaller units of text recur in numerous locales throughout the Hebrew Bible. An example of such reuse is the repetition of the circumstances surrounding Joshua's death in both Josh 24:28–31 and Judg 2:6–9. These repetitions of texts point to the reuse or selection of these units and demonstrate innertextuality and the composition of biblical texts.

The notion of arrangement is likewise observed in the placement of smaller units of text within that of a larger whole. Whether law codes, small narratives, poetry, repeated episodes, or even smaller repetitions, an author arranges texts in order to achieve a certain structure. This structure or form of the text produces a certain effect on the reader. A different arrangement of textual units would likewise create a distinct effect or message. Arrangement is important for the communication of a message because of the manner in which a reader seeks to understand individual narratives in light of the whole text.[71] Imagine that Genesis 3 were placed

---

70. Fohrer, *Exegese des Alten Testaments*, 143–47.

71. Hirsch, *Validity in Interpretation*, 85–88, 258–59. For this notion applied to bibli-

immediately after the narrative of the golden calf. What new associations would result because of this hypothetical placement? Such considerations demonstrate the often-overlooked significance of arrangement.

Arrangement has important ramifications for the notion of inner-textuality. If the selected units are arranged in such a way that recurring elements are able to easily interface with one another, then an emphasis is quickly noted. Moreover, if the similar units are distributed throughout an entire larger unit, then the notion of innertextuality can aptly be used to describe the strategy employed by the author.

The notion of adaptation suggests a modification of a particular unit in order to fit within the desired arrangement. Textual units were possibly abbreviated or configured to fit with other textual units based on a need within the whole. Consequently, the author matched the abbreviated unit with the context in a way that has the desired effect. The following examination of Exodus 32 and Deuteronomy 9 will demonstrate how an adaptation of the clausal structures between Exod 32:20 and Deut 9:21 produces an emphasis upon the sin of the production of the golden calf.

The notion of writing involves an original formation of textual units. Although an author frequently utilizes smaller units of text and adapts those to his purpose, at times he generates new textual units. These new units might be on the scale of a letter or of a verbal, phrasal, or longer unit that would communicate the desired effect. Such original formation appears to be at work in the minor variations of otherwise verbatim quotations in the book of Chronicles.

At all times, any of these four means (selection, arrangement, adaptation, and writing) should fit within and correspond to the work as a whole. Composition results from the combination of smaller units into a larger whole. Innertextuality serves to connect smaller units into a composition by means of formal linguistic elements. Because composition involves texts distributed throughout the entire textual whole, a compositional approach should appeal to a greater amount of the data in a work. If a composition can be demonstrated, features that evince a composition should provide a more certain footing on which to base an interpretation of the work as a whole.

---

cal texts, see Sailhamer, *Old Testament Theology*, 213–14.

Composition and Meaning

This section will relate the composition of biblical narratives to the notion of meaning. It will show how selection, arrangement, adaptation, and writing contribute to a construction of meaning. In light of the processes of selection and arrangement, a composition can be detected through recurring formal characteristics distributed throughout an entire textual whole. A recurring textual unit may reveal a similar source or origin and may actually unveil the compositional process. A textual unit can be on the scale of linguistic signs, terms, phrases, clauses, sentences, or even paragraphs. The linguistic similarities between any two (or more) units may demonstrate the use of an independent textual unit in one of those two (or more) locales within a work. Moreover, the linguistic similarities may be due to the fact that this particular unit was generated for two (or more) places within a larger whole. In any case, when a similar textual unit is used, it may evince intentionality in its usage. Within the reused material, not only may the similarities be indicative of intentionality, but the dissimilarities become important as well.

From the perspective of this textual model, a number of smaller units can be utilized and arranged to form a whole. If it can be shown that a recurring textual unit likely existed independently, existed within another text, or was generated for two (or more) places within a larger whole, then the notion of selection is demonstrated. This component could be illustrated by reference to building blocks inserted and removed based on the edifice that is to be constructed. Depending on the purpose of an entire edifice, a particular block is chosen. Certain blocks are replicated because they are needed more often while other blocks are rarely used. One can also discern the significance of the arrangement of units in order to produce the desired effect. Units of text are able to be viewed in similar fashion. Some linguistic units are used often. When similar linguistic units are observed in different contexts, it may reveal the compositional activity.

Furthermore, an author may use a textual unit and then comment on that unit through the linking together, that is, the reuse of that same unit at another place within the larger composition. This understanding is sometimes spoken of as dependence on an earlier tradition. The complexity of this notion, moreover, has to do with the inadequacy to show which text alludes to the other. Although at times the direction of dependence can be detected, it is often difficult to do so. The more important consideration in a compositional unity is the connection between two texts that reveals the compositional activity and intimates the purpose for the connected textual units. In a unified textual work, the direction of dependence is not necessary to know, because it is a single work that is being examined.

In a compositional unity, the one responsible for composing the work out of these smaller textual units is not, by means of innertextuality, linguistically depending on or alluding to a textual unit used earlier within that compositional unity. Quotation and allusion are used for distinct purposes and are not in view here.[72] The author of this compositional unity is not by means of quotation or allusion linking his work with a previously written work. There is no trajectory of meaning, signaled by similar content, with which an author seeks to align the work. Rather, the author has fashioned the work by selecting, arranging, adapting, and writing the textual units into a structured and meaningful whole. In such a construction, the author is composing a new text. He may well be receiving certain traditional texts, commenting on them, and clarifying their meaning; but in the process of composition, he is authoring. An author constructs a framework and expresses a message through his composition of texts.

This manner of composition and its effects can be seen from the perspective of genre. Literary theorists acknowledge that genre is not simply a classification of texts. Rather, genre touches the very heart of the communication process. In the book *Kinds of Literature: An Introduction to the Theory of Genres and* Modes, Alastair Fowler writes,

> Every work of literature belongs to at least one genre. Indeed, it is sure to have a significant generic element. For genre has quite a different relation to creativity from the one usually supposed, whereby it is little more than a restraint upon spontaneous expression. Rightly understood, it is so far from being a mere curb on expression that it makes the expressiveness of literary works possible. Their relation to the genres they embody is not one of passive membership but of active modulation. Such modulation communicates. And it probably has a communicative value far greater than we can ever be directly aware of.[73]

72. Sommer, *A Prophet Reads Scripture*, 6–30.
73. Fowler, *Kinds of Literature*, 21.

The notion of genre extends beyond recognizing distinctions between types of literature to constituting the production of it. An author uses conventions of literature with which he is familiar in order to communicate. In the process he assimilates other genres in order to communicate. Moreover, he extends the genre in order to match his own individual purposes and characteristics.[74] An example of this type of genre extension can be seen in the early chapters of Genesis. It appears that the author has assimilated types of literature such as genealogy, flood narrative, and poetry into a larger unit. In so doing, he has created an individual account of creation. Although other creation accounts exist that have similarities, this one is unique because of the compositional-like process (i.e., selection, arrangement, adaptation, and writing in order to fit within a larger whole). In this case, the assimilation of other genre types carries with it implications for selection and arrangement. Genre extension may be a type of adaptation and writing. Consequently, even though an author uses familiar types, he constructs a distinct meaning because of his distinct assimilation and extension of those and other types.

This work attempts to extend this process of production of literature to the level of clauses, phrases, and words. An author composes in a similar fashion. He selects, arranges, adapts, and writes texts so that they cohere within a larger whole. An author may construct a meaning in part by associating certain texts with one another. This may produce an effect upon the reader because of the recognition of previous uses and contexts.

In his article "Some Observations on the Analysis of Structure in Biblical Narrative," Bar-Efrat attempted to understand an author's structure because of his expectation of a certain manner of structure.[75] In certain cases, structure was dependent on the recurrence of linguistic features. This recurrence of linguistic features became an expectation, a conception of genre, which Bar-Efrat shared with the author. Through this shared expectation, Bar-Efrat gained a particular understanding of the narrative.

In a similar manner, James Muilenburg stressed the importance of form and linguistic patterns to discern an author's meaning. In his article, "Form Criticism and Beyond," Muilenburg states, "For the more deeply one penetrates the formulations as they have been transmitted to us, the

---

74. Ibid, 32, 42–49, 153–56.
75. Bar-Efrat, "Some Observations on the Analysis of Structure."

more sensitive he is to the roles which words and motifs play in a composition; the more he concentrates on the ways in which thought has been woven into linguistic patterns, the better able he is to think the thoughts of the biblical writer after him."[76] Muilenburg seems intent on helping scholarship move beyond the bare content of a text, what one could refer to as mere denotation, to a richer message for which reason the author was communicating. Muilenburg continues, "A responsible and proper articulation of the words in their linguistic patterns and in their precise formulations will reveal to us the texture and fabric of the writer's thought, not only what it is that he thinks, but as he thinks it."[77] Muilenberg helps us focus on the linguistic patterns and formulations in order to grasp the intention.

Muilenburg's article initiated an approach to Old Testament studies known as rhetorical criticism.[78] Rhetorical criticism was interested in "understanding the nature of Hebrew literary composition, in exhibiting the structural patterns that are employed for the fashioning of a literary unit, whether in poetry or in prose, and in discerning the many and various devices by which the predications are formulated and ordered into a unified whole."[79] Rhetorical criticism went beyond an understanding of the form itself to an understanding of the entire text in which a form was woven.

Muilenburg's approach was interested in the "linguistic patterns" and "precise formulations." These patterns and formulations revealed the structure in which an author used certain forms and communicated a message. Authors did this by arranging pericopes and combining them into larger wholes. This view has particular force for the notion of arrangement. In a critique of Muilenburg and rhetorical criticism, Barton assesses this aspect of the deliberate organization of parts. Concerning Muilenburg's commentary on Isaiah, he writes, "Muilenburg sees the pericopes as also arranged in a deliberate way . . . These may once have been two separate oracles; but as they stand, they are mutually illuminating, and to such an extent that the ordering looks deliberate."[80] Moreover, the

---

76. Muilenburg, "Form Criticism and Beyond," 7.

77. Ibid.

78. Barton, *Reading the Old Testament*, 199–204.

79. Muilenburg, "Form Criticism and Beyond," 8.

80. Barton, *Reading the Old Testament*, 200–201.

patterns and formulations involved repetition which aided the reader. On nearly every page in the remainder of his article, Muilenburg demonstrates how recurring linguistic signs indicate structure and have implications for meaning.[81] Innertextuality functions in much the same manner through recurring linguistic signs. These signs compose textual units, which serve to unite texts into larger wholes.

CRITERIA OF ASSOCIATION[82]

This chapter has shown that recurring textual units indicate possible compositional activity. In order to determine whether that recurring textual unit is intentional or coincidental, one must establish criteria in order to adjudicate the nature of the recurrence. This section will propose the following criteria of association: similar terminology, similar syntax, similar narrative features, similar thematic contexts, similar sequence of events, repetition of structure, contextual awareness, breaking a recognizable pattern, and shifting connotation. These criteria will be used to demonstrate innertextual passages and their inclusion in a compositional framework. As stated above, a recurrence of a textual unit is an element that may indicate a composition. Moreover, Eissfeldt demonstrated that the horizon of a unit can be seen by the recurrence of similar elements.[83] A composer brings textual pieces into a larger whole by reusing certain textual units. How can this be detected? How can this type of compositional activity be seen in a larger work? The similarities between two or more units betray their intentional association.

Before one can adjudicate innertextuality and the resulting composition, a recurrence of textual units must exist distributed throughout the entirety of the unit. While not everyone would describe this type of linguistic recurrence as compositional activity, the observations of other scholars concerning analogous elements aids the detection of association between two texts.

The notion of one text relating to another is not new. Hebrew writers from the earliest times associated one text with another in a prolific

---

81. Muilenburg, "Form Criticism and Beyond," 10, 11, 13, 14, 15, 16, 17.

82. The term *association* rather than *dependence* is used because the objective within a textual unity is not to discover which text is alluding or depending on the other, but whether the two texts are intentionally associated with each other.

83. Eissfeldt, "Die kleinste literarische Einheit."

manner. One can hardly deny the impact of inter-relationships upon the formation of the Bible.[84] Furthermore, early Christian scholars at once seized upon the New Testament's use of the Old Testament and attempted to elucidate the meaning of the relationship between the two texts.[85] However, it is not primarily the relationship of the Old Testament to the New Testament that should be considered. Fishbane, Seeligmann, and others have shown that a first consideration is the association between Old Testament texts themselves and even relationships between passages within the same book. How can one discern the manner of the relationship? Some have suggested diachronic concerns are secondary or even unimportant.

Within biblical studies and general literary theory, there has been a certain shift towards poststructuralist or reader-response interpretations, which would remove the need to trace the linkage to intentionality.[86] A strong assortment of voices, however, wants to ground the interpretive choices in a demonstrable basis.[87] While some may argue whether the grounds are traced to an author or redactor, the aims of interpretation are focused in a similar direction; this recurrence of linguistic elements, that is, innertextuality, should be grounded in criteria of association.[88]

Although criteria of association have been solicited, they have been slow in coming. What often seems to be the case is that certain criteria are set forth based on the particular passage or book a person is examining. There have been few significant theoretical discussions of literary relationship or dependence in the Hebrew Bible or within the entire

---

84. Fishbane, *Biblical Interpretation*; Seeligmann, "Voraussetzungen der Midrasch-exegese," 152–81.

85. For one example among many, see Origen, *Commentary on the Epistle to the Romans*, 237–78.

86. Cf. Exum and Clines, *New Literary Criticism*. See also a move toward poststructuralism in Nielsen, "Intertextuality and Hebrew Bible," 17–31.

87. For those outside biblical studies who want to tie the relationship between two texts to intentionality, see Chandler, "Romantic Allusiveness," 460–66, 486–87; Kronfeld, "Allusion," 137–40; and Perri, "On Alluding," 289–307.

88. Sailhamer, *Introduction to Old Testament Theology*, 213; Hurvitz, *A Linguistic Study*, 7; Mettinger, "Intertextuality," 262; Charlesworth, "Intertextuality," 203; Noble, "Esau, Tamar, and Joseph," 220, 227–28; Sommer, "Exegesis, Allusion and Intertextuality in the Hebrew Bible," 484–85; Longenecker, *Biblical Exegesis*, xx–xviii, who quotes Fishbane's criteria; Fishbane, *Biblical Interpretation*, 42–43, 288–89, 291; Hays, *Echoes of Scripture*, 25–33.

Christian canon.[89] Criteria are offered in passing, but what remains to be done is a theoretical discussion of the phenomena, basic analysis of the phenomena, and methodological controls.[90]

One could argue, however, that there is good reason why the only discussion of criteria involves individual passages. Elements are sought betraying an intentional connection between units of texts. A case-by-case basis is essential, and a thorough examination would produce volumes. These elements cannot be merely the usage of a common term. The issues are complex, and therefore the process of determining association must go beyond a simple comparison of words to something that provides evidence that one unit of text was intentionally linked with another one. The possibilities that would betray such a practice are practically unlimited. In an article dealing with the allusion of one text to another, Ben Sommer notes that this complexity should not frighten away attempts to do this. He says, "Weighing such evidence and hence identifying allusions constitutes an art, not a science, but the recognition that the study of literary history is no science should provoke neither surprise nor despair."[91] Methodology becomes increasingly important in such an enterprise. Criteria should demonstrate an intentional association of texts.

As with many sciences, one is not looking for a single condition to establish an indubitable case. Accumulated evidence can be brought to bear, which will further heighten the probability of innertextuality. It is often the accumulation of individual conditions that conveys probability. As Mark Reasoner has said, "One criterion is not meant to be viewed as a single artery, making a body member dependent on the heart. Rather, each criterion could be pictured as one part of a capillary bed which in its entirety provides nutrients for the dependent member of the body."[92] Often, the more criteria one can establish for a connection between texts, the better the case for an intentional linkage.

The task remains to set forth a number of criteria that will ascertain an intentional connection between texts. To do this, this section will draw on examples of criteria that others have set forth. Usually the first notice of a perceived relationship comes when two texts use the same word or

---

89. Fishbane, *Biblical Interpretation*. See also Schultz, *Search for Quotation*.

90. See Ben-Porat, "The Poetics of Literary Allusion," 105–28.

91. Sommer, "Exegesis, Allusion and Intertextuality in the Hebrew Bible," 485–86.

92. Reasoner, "Relationship of Three Old Testament Woman-at-the-Well Texts," 35.

words. Caution must be taken if the term is a common word in biblical Hebrew.[93] If the word or phrase is rare, however, the likelihood of intentional association is increased.[94] Sommer discusses the probability of allusion if a text has already displayed a certain connection to another text, or if the alluding text consistently alters the structure of a given phrase or clause.[95] Although caution must be taken, any similar syntactical construction can indicate an intentional association.[96]

Moreover, if a particular word in the perceived innertextuality is used dissimilarly to how it is employed elsewhere in the book, but is used in a similar manner to how it is used in the analogous textual unit, an intentional connection is likely.[97] The same example of dissimilar understanding can be applied to syntactical analysis.[98]

Although every case must be handled individually, often the greater the number of similar points of contact between the two passages, the greater the likelihood of connection. Other literary devices—such as narrative structuring, narrative characterization, dialogue, and point of view—may indicate an intentional connection when shown to be used in similar fashion.[99] Again, if these elements that connect the passages are used similarly in the related texts but dissimilarly from how they are otherwise used in the book, an intentional connection is probable.

Furthermore, the occurrence of similar events or themes can indicate a connection. When the same events or themes (in particular, the same sequence of events or themes) take place in both passages, a connection is likely. Normally, similar terminology is also present in these cases. Respective to the events, the subject and object, the characterization of the action, and the consequences of the action may flow in like direction

---

93. There is also the question of traditional "vocabulary clusters." Sommer, "Exegesis, Allusion and Intertextuality in the Hebrew Bible," 484. For a similar concern, see Fishbane, *Biblical Interpretation*, 288–89.

94. Sommer, "Exegesis, Allusion and Intertextuality in the Hebrew Bible," 485; Schultz, *The Search for Quotation*, 222–24.

95. Sommer, ibid.

96. Lawson, "Literary Relationship," 30; Reasoner, "Relationship," 39.

97. Lawson, "Literary Relationship," 29; Reasoner, "Relationship," 37.

98. Lawson, "Literary Relationship," 29; Reasoner, "Relationship," 37.

99. Reasoner, "Relationship," 39–42.

in both texts.[100] Otherwise, the likelihood of intentional association possibly decreases.[101]

Another factor that evinces literary association involves a text's following another text's rhetorical structure rather than straightforward narrative sequence. For example, a parallel structure between narratives could exist in a larger textual unit. If a text is composed in light of this design rather than following the verbatim details in the unit, the linkage between texts becomes apparent.[102]

Another indication of connection can be detected in what Umberto Cassuto calls the "allusive character" of certain phraseology.[103] Here Cassuto refers to the character of certain texts either explicitly or implicitly to refer to another text. An explicit reference might be the use of a definite article to show the awareness of the referenced passage or object.[104] An implicit reference would be the rephrasing or reinterpretation of material, making it likely that the reference would be in one direction. Cassuto mentions this occurrence in connection with poetic language. It is common enough for an author to go from a simple description to poetic language without implying literary dependence. If one moves, however, from poetic description to simple language, it is difficult to remove the poetic flair, and intentional association, and even dependence, is detected.[105] In a similar manner, Schultz notes that a variation between otherwise similar texts may indicate a contextual awareness of the quoted text. He asserts that often this feature, in contrast with exact quotation, indicates dependence.[106]

With all of these criteria, the literary context should be considered and becomes an additional, corroborative criterion that heightens the likelihood of a connection. Without a similar context, the related elements may be related in an innerbiblical relationship where the similarities are the result of various causes. In this type of relationship, the common words or phrases might be similar but not necessarily intentionally connected.

---

100. Lawson, "Literary Relationship," 28.

101. See Noble, "Esau, Tamar, and Joseph," 222–32.

102. See Sailhamer, "Hosea 11:1 and Matthew 2:15," 87–96.

103. Cassuto, *Biblical and Oriental Studies*, 1:94.

104. Ibid.

105. Ibid.

106. Schultz, *Search for Quotation*, 224–28.

Moreover, the related elements might not contribute to the larger whole in which they are embedded. In certain respects, this is what Fishbane demonstrates in his book.[107] Moreover, Fohrer explains a recurring pattern of elements as a redactional gloss if it is not related to the whole of the book.[108] Similarities in linguistic elements limited to an immediate context are inconsistent with the notion of innertextuality described in this chapter.

Another criterion of innertextuality involves a recognizable textual unit: for example, a rhetorical feature such as an acrostic or typical *Gattung*. When these recognizable forms are subsequently missing an element or have an additional feature, an intentional relationship between the typical usage of the form and its utilization is detected.[109] An additional example involving a recognizable unit concerns a subsequent recurrence of that textual unit. When that subsequent usage of the textual unit alters the pattern in a minor way, it breaks the recognizable unit and consequently may signal an intentional connection.

A connection is also detected by a motif or term that shifts in connotation. Terminology or phrases that begin to take on a larger meaning betray a purposeful association. Ezek 20:33–34 may serve as an example of such a shift in connotation. In Ezek 20:33–34 twice one reads of the phrase "mighty hand and outstretched arm." It is used in 20:34 in connection with the eschatological gathering of Israel from the nations. This phrase certainly refers to God's power in delivering the Israelites from Egypt. It is used often in the book of Deuteronomy in reference to God's deliverance of Israel from Egypt (Deut 4:34; 5:15; 7:19; 9:29; 11:2; and 26:8) as well as in other books of the Hebrew Bible. Its usage in Ezekiel 20, however, no longer connotes the exodus from Egypt but rather the exodus when God will deliver them from the nations. The subsequent verses in Ezekiel 20 confirm this understanding.

These criteria indicate a connection between textual units. When such a link between two or more passages is proven, it demonstrates an intentional connection. Furthermore, when connected texts are dis-

---

107. Fishbane, *Biblical Interpretation*; Cf. Seeligmann, "Voraussetzungen der Midraschexegese," 153–67; Cassuto, *Biblical and Oriental Studies*, 1:87–88.

108. Fohrer, *Exegese des Alten Testaments*, 143–47.

109. This criterion was suggested by John Sailhamer in a PhD seminar in March of 2006, Southeastern Baptist Theological Seminary concerning a discussion of Habakkuk 3.

tributed throughout a larger whole, innertextuality is demonstrated. In such a case, the innertextuality constitutes a compositional strategy. This strategy in turn reveals the framework through which an author is able to communicate a message.

This chapter defined innertextuality and related the phenomenon to the notion of composition. The chapter also established a set of criteria by which to determine an intentional connection between related passages. The following chapter will apply these criteria to Exod 32:7–20 and Deut 9:12–21. It will seek to demonstrate a possible innertextual relationship between the two passages.

TABLE 1. Criteria to Establish Intentional Connection and Innertextuality

1. Similar terminology

2. Similar syntax

3. Similar narrative features

4. Similar thematic contexts

5. Similar sequence of events

6. Repetition of structure

7. Contextual awareness[110]

8. Breaking a recognizable pattern

9. Shifting connotation

---

110. Schultz, *Search for Quotation*, 223–33.

2

Analyzing the Relationship between Exodus 32:7–20 and Deuteronomy 9:12–21

OLD TESTAMENT SCHOLARS ACKNOWLEDGE that a relationship exists between the narrative of the golden calf in Exodus 32 and the narrative of the golden calf in Deuteronomy 9.[1] The question is what type of relationship is it? This chapter will demonstrate a likely innertextual connection between Exod 32:7–20 and Deut 9:12–21. The chapter will apply criteria of association in an analysis of the two passages.

COMPARISON OF EXODUS 32:7–20 AND DEUTERONOMY 9:12–21

This section will show a comparison of Exod 32:7–20 and Deut 9:12–21. Figure 1 illustrates the makeup of the relationship between Exod 32:7–20 and Deut 9:12–21. Material that is identical between the two passages corresponds to the material in the parallel column and is not underlined. If there is no material in the parallel column then the two passages diverge at those points. Material which is underlined represents minor syntactical or lexical divergence.

Figure 1 establishes to a high degree of probability that the two passages were composed in relationship to one another and intentionally connected. Every place of agreement between the two passages meets: 1) criterion 1, similar terminology; 2) criterion 2, similar syntax; 3) criterion 4, similar context. Moreover, at various places which will be discussed below, formal elements between the two passages also meet: 1) criterion 3, similar narrative features; 2) criterion 5, sequence of events; 3) criterion 7, contextual awareness; and 4) criterion 8, breaking a recognizable pattern.

1. To my knowledge, the most recent analysis of passages involving the golden calf is Dozeman, "Composition of Ex 32," 175–89 and Lindqvist, *Sin at Sinai*.

This comparison of Exod 32:7–20 and Deut 9:12–21 demonstrates that the identical terminological and clausal constructions, thematic contexts, sequence of events, and contextual awareness which exists between these passages cannot be accidental and would not be without purpose in the final shape of the Pentateuch. Moreover, the linguistic agreement between the two passages shows the likelihood that an innertextual relationship exists between them. Chapter Three will discuss the likelihood of innertextuality between these two passages and others distributed throughout the Pentateuch.

It is possible that either Exod 32:7–20 or Deut 9:12–21 served as the archetype for the other. Furthermore, it is possible that both passages could be depending on another similar source.[2] A direction of dependence, however, is not the focus of this analysis. Figure 1 and the catalogue of clauses, phrases, and terminology demonstrate that within the final shape of the Pentateuch, these two passages were composed in relationship to one another. This analysis attempts to discern the manner of that relationship and its coherence within the compositional strategies of the Pentateuch.

CATALOGUE OF CLAUSES, PHRASES, AND TERMINOLOGY

Figure 1 demonstrates the similar, formal, linguistic elements between Exod 32:7–20 and Deut 9:12–21. These parallel elements evince a relationship between the two passages, which extends beyond coincidence. What was the purpose of this relationship? How can the theological intentions be discerned in the relationship between the two passages? The analysis below will catalogue the clauses in order to show the intentional connection and demonstrate the likelihood of innertextuality. This catalogue will also provide the basis from which to discern the theological intentions in the selection, arrangement, or adaptation of textual units. The lists of clauses convey the following: material identical in both narrative accounts; material identical in both accounts except for grammatical person; material identical in both accounts except for an additional word (some of which also alter grammatical person); material approximately corresponding to the parallel account but varying slightly in lexeme, syn-

---

2. For a discussion of dependence and redactional strata, see Schmitt, "Erzählung vom Goldenen Kalb," 235–48; Van Seters, *Life of Moses*, 290–318; Hyatt, *Exodus*, 301; Hahn, "*Goldene Kalb,* " 140; Aurelius, *Fürbitter Israels*, 57–90; Scharbert, *Exodus*, 120–25; Boorer, *Promise of the Land as Oath*, 203–325.

Figure 1. Textual alignment of Exod 32:7–20 and Deut 9: 12–21[3]

Exod 32:7–20	Deut 9:12–21
⁷ וַיְדַבֵּר יהוה אֶל־מֹשֶׁה לֶךְ־רֵד כִּי שִׁחֵת עַמְּךָ אֲשֶׁר הֶעֱלֵיתָ מֵאֶרֶץ מִצְרָיִם: ⁸ סָרוּ מַהֵר מִן־הַדֶּרֶךְ אֲשֶׁר צִוִּיתִם עָשׂוּ לָהֶם עֵגֶל מַסֵּכָה וַיִּשְׁתַּחֲווּ־לוֹ וַיִּזְבְּחוּ־לוֹ וַיֹּאמְרוּ אֵלֶּה אֱלֹהֶיךָ יִשְׂרָאֵל אֲשֶׁר הֶעֱלוּךָ מֵאֶרֶץ מִצְרָיִם: ⁹ וַיֹּאמֶר יהוה אֶל־מֹשֶׁה רָאִיתִי אֶת־הָעָם הַזֶּה וְהִנֵּה עַם־קְשֵׁה־עֹרֶף הוּא: ¹⁰ וְעַתָּה הַנִּיחָה לִּי וְיִחַר־אַפִּי בָהֶם וַאֲכַלֵּם וְאֶעֱשֶׂה אוֹתְךָ לְגוֹי גָּדוֹל: ¹¹ וַיְחַל מֹשֶׁה אֶת־פְּנֵי יהוה אֱלֹהָיו וַיֹּאמֶר לָמָה יהוה יֶחֱרֶה אַפְּךָ בְּעַמֶּךָ אֲשֶׁר הוֹצֵאתָ מֵאֶרֶץ מִצְרַיִם בְּכֹחַ גָּדוֹל וּבְיָד חֲזָקָה: ¹² לָמָּה יֹאמְרוּ מִצְרַיִם לֵאמֹר בְּרָעָה הוֹצִיאָם לַהֲרֹג אֹתָם בֶּהָרִים וּלְכַלֹּתָם מֵעַל פְּנֵי הָאֲדָמָה שׁוּב מֵחֲרוֹן אַפֶּךָ וְהִנָּחֵם עַל־הָרָעָה לְעַמֶּךָ: ¹³ זְכֹר לְאַבְרָהָם לְיִצְחָק וּלְיִשְׂרָאֵל עֲבָדֶיךָ אֲשֶׁר נִשְׁבַּעְתָּ לָהֶם בָּךְ וַתְּדַבֵּר אֲלֵהֶם אַרְבֶּה אֶת־זַרְעֲכֶם כְּכוֹכְבֵי הַשָּׁמָיִם וְכָל־הָאָרֶץ הַזֹּאת אֲשֶׁר אָמַרְתִּי אֶתֵּן לְזַרְעֲכֶם וְנָחֲלוּ לְעֹלָם: ¹⁴ וַיִּנָּחֶם יהוה עַל־הָרָעָה אֲשֶׁר דִּבֶּר לַעֲשׂוֹת לְעַמּוֹ: פ ¹⁵ וַיִּפֶן וַיֵּרֶד מֹשֶׁה מִן־הָהָר וּשְׁנֵי לֻחֹת הָעֵדֻת בְּיָדוֹ לֻחֹת כְּתֻבִים מִשְּׁנֵי עֶבְרֵיהֶם מִזֶּה וּמִזֶּה הֵם כְּתֻבִים:	¹² וַיֹּאמֶר יהוה אֵלַי קוּם רֵד מַהֵר מִזֶּה כִּי שִׁחֵת עַמְּךָ אֲשֶׁר הוֹצֵאתָ מִמִּצְרָיִם סָרוּ מַהֵר מִן־הַדֶּרֶךְ אֲשֶׁר צִוִּיתִם עָשׂוּ לָהֶם מַסֵּכָה: ¹³ וַיֹּאמֶר יהוה אֵלַי לֵאמֹר רָאִיתִי אֶת־הָעָם הַזֶּה וְהִנֵּה עַם־קְשֵׁה־עֹרֶף הוּא: ¹⁴ הֶרֶף מִמֶּנִּי וְאַשְׁמִידֵם וְאֶמְחֶה אֶת־שְׁמָם מִתַּחַת הַשָּׁמָיִם וְאֶעֱשֶׂה אוֹתְךָ לְגוֹי־ עָצוּם וָרָב מִמֶּנּוּ: ¹⁵ וָאֵפֶן וָאֵרֵד מִן־הָהָר וְהָהָר בֹּעֵר בָּאֵשׁ וּשְׁנֵי לֻחֹת הַבְּרִית עַל שְׁתֵּי יָדָי:

3. The Hebrew text is from Bibleworks.7

Exodus 32:7–20	Deuteronomy 9:12–21
16 והלחת מעשה אלהים המה	
והמכתב מכתב אלהים הוא	
חרות על־הלחת: 17 וישמע	
יהושע את־קול העם ברעה	
ויאמר אל־משה קול מלחמה	
במחנה: 18 ויאמר אין קול	
ענות גבורה ואין קול ענות	
חלושה קול ענות אנכי שמע:	
19 ויהי כאשר קרב אל־המחנה	
וירא	16 וארא והנה חטאתם ליהוה
את־העגל	אלהיכם עשיתם לכם עגל מסכה
	סרתם מהר מן־הדרך אשר־צוה
	יהוה אתכם:
	17 ואתפש בשני הלחת ואשלכם
ומחלת ויחר־אף משה	מעל שתי ידי
וישלך	ואשברם
מידו את־הלחת וישבר אתם	לעיניכם: 18 ואתנפל לפני יהוה
תחת ההר:	כראשנה ארבעים יום וארבעים
	לילה לחם לא אכלתי ומים לא
	שתיתי על כל־חטאתכם אשר
	חטאתם לעשות הרע בעיני יהוה
	להכעיסו: 19 כי יגרתי מפני האף
	והחמה אשר קצף יהוה עליכם
	להשמיד אתכם וישמע יהוה
	אלי גם בפעם ההוא: 20 ובאהרן
	התאנף יהוה מאד להשמידו
	ואתפלל גם־בעד אהרן בעת
	ההוא: 21 ואת־חטאתכם אשר־עשיתם
20 ויקח את־העגל אשר עשו	את־העגל לקחתי
וישרף באש	ואשרף אתו באש ואכת אתו
ויטחן עד אשר־דק	טחון היטב עד אשר־דק לעפר
ויזר על־פני המים	ואשלך את־עפרו אל־הנחל
וישק את־בני ישראל:	הירד מן־ההר:

Exodus 32:7–20[4]	Deuteronomy 9:12–21
7. And the Lord <u>said</u> to <u>Moses</u>, "<u>Go</u>, go down because your people whom you <u>brought up</u> from <u>the land</u> of Egypt have acted corruptly. 8. They turned quickly from the way which I commanded them. They made for themselves a calf, molten image. And they bowed down to it and they sacrificed to it and they said, 'These are your gods, Israel who brought you up from the land of Egypt.'"	12. And the Lord <u>said</u> to <u>me</u>, "<u>Arise</u>, go down quickly from here because your people whom you <u>brought out</u> from Egypt have acted corruptly. They turned quickly from the way which I commanded them. They made for themselves a molten image.
9. And the Lord said to <u>Moses</u>, "I have seen this people and behold, they are a stiff-necked people. 10. And now, <u>let me alone</u> and my anger will burn against them and I will <u>destroy</u> them and I will make you into a <u>great</u> nation. 11. And Moses entreated the Lord his God and he said, "Why, Lord, does your anger burn against your people whom you brought out from the land of Egypt with great strength and with a strong hand? 12. Why should the Egyptians speak, saying, 'With harmful intent he brought them out to slay them in the mountains and to destroy them from upon the face of the land.' Return from your burning anger and repent over the harm concerning your people. 13. Remember Abraham, Isaac, and Israel, your servants whom you swore to them by yourself and you said to them, 'I will multiply your seed as the stars of the heavens' and all this land which I said 'I will give	13. And the Lord said to <u>me</u>, saying, "I have seen this people and behold, they are a stiff-necked people. 14. <u>Let me alone</u> and I will <u>destroy</u> them and I will wipe their name from under the heavens and I will make you into a more <u>vast</u> and numerous nation than they.

4. Author's translation throughout.

to your offspring and they will possess
it forever.'" 14. And the Lord repented
concerning the harm which he
spoke about doing to his people. 15. And
Moses turned and he went down from
the mountain
            and the two tablets of the
testimony were   in his hands, tablets
written on both sides, they were written
on one side and on the other. 16. And
the tablets were the work of God and the
writing was the writing of God engraved
upon the tablets. 17. And Joshua heard
the sound of the people as they shouted
and he said to Moses, "The sound of war
is in the camp." 18. And he said, "It is
not the sound of the shout of strength
and it is not the sound of the shout of
weakness; the sound of shouting I am
hearing. 19. And it happened when he
drew near to the camp
and he saw

            the calf

                        and
the dancing that the anger of Moses
burned
and he cast   the tablets from   his
hands and he broke them at the bottom
of the mountain.

15. And
I turned and I went down from the
mountain and the mountain was burning with fire and the two tablets of the
covenant were in both of my hands.

16. And I looked and behold, you sinned
against the Lord your God; you made
for yourselves a calf, a molten image. You
turned quickly from the way which the
Lord commanded you.

17. And I took hold of the two tablets and I cast them   from the two
of my hands and I broke them before
your eyes. 18. And I fell before the Lord
as at first, forty days and forty nights,
I neither ate bread nor drank water
because of all your sin which you committed to do evil in the eyes of the Lord
to provoke him to anger. 19. Because I
feared the anger and wrath which the
Lord was enraged over you to destroy

	you and the Lord listened to me also at that time. 20. And against Aaron the Lord was angered enough to destroy him and I prayed also on behalf of Aaron at that time. 21. And your sin when you made
20. And <u>he</u> took the calf which <u>they</u> had made and <u>he</u> burned it with fire and <u>he</u> ground it until it was crushed and <u>he scattered</u> it <u>up</u>on the <u>water</u> and he made the sons of Israel drink it.	the golden calf, <u>I</u> took it and <u>I</u> burned it with fire and I beat it, grind<u>ing</u> it thoroughly until it was crushed to dust and <u>I cast</u> its dust <u>to</u> the stream coming down from the mountain.

tax, or grammatical person; material limited to Exod 32:7–20; and material limited to Deut 9:12–20.

The clauses identical in both accounts are:

- Exod 32:7d//Deut 9:12d: כִּי שִׁחֵת עַמְּךָ "because your people are acting ruinously"
- Exod 32:8a//Deut 9:12–13: סָרוּ מַהֵר מִן־הַדֶּרֶךְ "They turned aside quickly from the way"
- Exod 32:8b//Deut 9:12g: אֲשֶׁר צִוִּיתִם "Which I commanded them"
- Exod 32:9b//Deut 9:13c: רָאִיתִי אֶת־הָעָם הַזֶּה "I have seen this people"
- Exod 32:9c//Deut 9:13c: וְהִנֵּה עַם־קְשֵׁה־עֹרֶף הוּא "And behold they are a stiff-necked people"
- Exod 32:20e//Deut 9:21e: עַד אֲשֶׁר־דָּק "until it was finely ground"

The clauses that are the same in both accounts except for grammatical person are:

- Exod 32:9a//Deut 9:13a: ... וַיֹּאמֶר יְהוָה אֶל "And the Lord spoke to Moses/me"
- Exod 32:15a//Deut 9:15a: ... וַיִּפֶן "And [Moses]/I turned"
- Exod 32:15b//Deut 9:15b: ... וַיֵּרֶד מֹשֶׁה מִן־הָהָר "And Moses/I went down from the mountain"

- Exod 32:19c//Deut 9:16a: ... וָאֵרֶא "And he/I saw"

- Exod 32:20b//Deut 9:21b: ... אֲשֶׁר עָשׂוּ "which they/you made"

The clauses that are the same in both accounts except for an additional word (some clauses also alter grammatical person) are

- Exod 32:8c//Deut 9:12c: עָשׂוּ לָהֶם [עֵגֶל] מַסֵּכָה (additional word in brackets) "They made for themselves a calf, a molten image/ molten image"

- Exod 32:20c//Deut 9:21c: ... בָּאֵשׁ [אֹתוֹ] וַיִּשְׂרֹף (additional word in brackets) And he/I burned it with fire"

The clauses that approximately correspond to the parallel account but vary slightly in lexeme, syntax, or grammatical person are:

- Exod 32:7a//Deut 9:12a: וַיְדַבֵּר יְהוָה אֶל־מֹשֶׁה "And the Lord spoke to Moses"//

- וַיֹּאמֶר יְהוָה אֵלַי "And the Lord spoke to me"

- Exod 32:7b,c//Deut 9:12b,c: לֶךְ־רֵד "go down"//קוּם רֵד "arise, go down"

- Exod 32: 7e//Deut 9:12e: [אֲשֶׁר הֶ[עֱלֵיתָ [מֵאֶרֶץ] מִצְרָיִם (additional word in brackets) "which you brought up from the land of Egypt"//אֲשֶׁר הוֹצֵאתָ מִמִּצְרָיִם "which you brought out from Egypt "

- Exod 32:10a//Deut 9:14a: [וְעַתָּה] הַנִּיחָה לִּי (additional word in brackets) "And now, leave me"//הֶרֶף מִמֶּנִּי "Leave me alone"

- Exod 32:10c//Deut 9:14b: וַאֲכַלֵּם "and I will destroy them"//וְאַשְׁמִידֵם "and I will destroy them"

- Exod 32:10d//Deut 9:14c: וְאֶעֱשֶׂה אוֹתְךָ לְגוֹי גָּדוֹל "And I will make you into a great nation"//וְאֶעֱשֶׂה אוֹתְךָ לְגוֹי־עָצוּם "And I will make you into a vast nation"

- Exod 32:15c//Deut 9:15d: וּשְׁנֵי לֻחֹת הָעֵדֻת בְּיָדוֹ "And the two tablets of the testimony were in his hand"//וּשְׁנֵי לֻחֹת הַבְּרִית עַל [שְׁתֵּי] יָדָי (additional word in brackets) "And the two tablets of the covenant were upon the two of my hands"

- Exod 32:19d//Deut 9:17b: וַיַּשְׁלֵךְ 5 מִיָּדָיו אֶת־הַלֻּחֹת "And he cast from his hands the tablets"//וָאַשְׁלִכֵם מֵעַל שְׁתֵּי יָדָי "And I cast them from upon the two of my hands"

- Exod 32:19e//Deut 9:17c: וַיְשַׁבֵּר אֹתָם תַּחַת הָהָר "And he broke them at the bottom of the mountain"//וָאֲשַׁבְּרֵם לְעֵינֵיכֶם "And I broke them before your eyes"

- Exod 32:20a//Deut 9:21a: וַיִּקַּח אֶת־הָעֵגֶל "And he took the calf"// אֶת־הָעֵגֶל לָקַחְתִּי [וְאֶת־חַטַּאתְכֶם] (additional word in brackets) "And your sin, the calf, I took"

- Exod 32:20d//Deut 9:21d: וַיִּטְחַן "And he ground"//וָאֶכֹּת אֹתוֹ טָחוֹן הֵיטֵב "And I beat it grinding it well"

- Exod 32:20–21//Deut 9:21–22: וַיִּזֶר עַל־פְּנֵי הַמַּיִם "And he scattered it upon the faces of the waters"//וָאַשְׁלִךְ אֶת־עֲפָרוֹ אֶל־הַנַּחַל הַיֹּרֵד מִן־הָהָר "And I cast its dust to the stream going down from the mountain"

The terms, phrases, or clauses limited to Exodus 32:7–20 are

- Exod 32:7: מֵאֶרֶץ "from the land"

- Exod 32:8: עֵגֶל "calf"

- Exod 32:8d–h: וַיִּשְׁתַּחֲווּ־לוֹ וַיִּזְבְּחוּ־לוֹ וַיֹּאמְרוּ אֵלֶּה אֱלֹהֶיךָ יִשְׂרָאֵל אֲשֶׁר הֶעֱלוּךָ

- מֵאֶרֶץ מִצְרָיִם: "And they worshipped it and sacrificed to it and they said, 'These are your gods, Israel, who brought you up from the land of Egypt.'"

- Exod 32:10: וְעַתָּה "And now"

- Exod 32:10b: וְיִחַר־אַפִּי בָהֶם "And my anger will burn against them"

- Exod 32:11–14: "And Moses entreated the Lord his God and said, 'Why, Lord, does your anger burn against your people whom you brought out from the land of Egypt with great strength and by a strong hand? Why should the Egyptians speak saying, 'With harmful intent he brought them out to slay them in the mountains and to destroy them from upon the face of the land.' Return from your burning anger and repent over the harm to your people. Remember Abraham, Isaac, and Israel, your servants whom you swore to them by yourself and you said to

---

5. Kethib-qere מְיָדָו מִיָּדָיו.

them, 'I will multiply your seed as the stars of the heavens and all this land which I said, 'I will give it to your seed and they will possess it forever.'" And the Lord repented over the evil which he spoke about doing to his people."

- Exod 32:15d–19b: "tablets written on both sides, they were written one side and on the other, and the tablets were the work of God, and the writing was the writing of God engraved upon the tablets. And Joshua heard the sound of the people as they shouted and he said to Moses, 'The sound of war is in the camp.' And he said, 'It is not the sound of the shout of strength and it is not the sound of the shout of weakness, the sound of shouting I am hearing.' And it happened when he drew near to the camp."

- Exod 32:19d: וּמְחֹלֹת וַיִּחַר־אַף מֹשֶׁה "and the dancing that the anger of Moses burned"

- Exod 32:19e: אֶת־הַלֻּחֹת "tablets"

- Exod 32:20g: וַיַּשְׁקְ אֶת־בְּנֵי יִשְׂרָאֵל "And he gave it to the sons of Israel to drink"

The terms, phrases, or clauses that are limited to Deut 9:12–21 are:

- Deut 9:12: מַהֵר מִזֶּה "quickly from this place"

- Deut 9:13: לֵאמֹר "saying"

- Deut 9:14c: וְאֶמְחֶה אֶת־שְׁמָם מִתַּחַת הַשָּׁמָיִם "And I will blot their name from under the heavens"

- Deut 9:14d: וְרָב מִמֶּנּוּ "and greater than they"

- Deut 9:15c: וְהָהָר בֹּעֵר בָּאֵשׁ "and the mountain was burning with fire"

- Deut 9:16b: וְהִנֵּה חֲטָאתֶם לַיהוָה אֱלֹהֵיכֶם עֲשִׂיתֶם לָכֶם עֵגֶל מַסֵּכָה סַרְתֶּם מַהֵר מִן־הַדֶּרֶךְ אֲשֶׁר־צִוָּה יְהוָה אֶתְכֶם: "And behold, you sinned against the Lord your God, you made for yourselves a molten calf, you turned quickly from the way which the Lord commanded you."

- Deut 9:17a: וָאֶתְפֹּשׂ בִּשְׁנֵי הַלֻּחֹת "and I lay hold of the two tablets"

- Deut 9:18–21a: "And I fell before the Lord as at first, forty days and forty nights; I neither ate bread nor did I drink water because of all your sin which you committed to do evil in the eyes of the Lord to provoke him to anger. Because I feared the anger and wrath which the Lord was enraged over you to destroy you and the Lord listened to me also at that time. And against Aaron the Lord was angered enough to destroy him and I prayed also on behalf of Aaron at that time. And your sin"

- Deut 9:21: אֹתוֹ (Direct Object marker) "it"

- Deut 9:21e: וָאֶכֹּת אֹתוֹ "and I beat it"

- Deut 9:21e: הֵיטֵב "thoroughly"

- Deut 9:21g: אֶת־עֲפָרוֹ "its dust"

Each of the clauses that fall into the following categories meet the criteria of similar terminology and syntax: 1) the clauses that are identical in both accounts; 2) the clauses that are the same in both accounts except for grammatical person; 3) the clauses that are the same in both accounts except for an additional word; and 4) the clauses that approximately correspond to the parallel account but slightly vary in lexeme or syntax or grammatical person. This material exhibits such close correspondence that within the final shape of the Pentateuch, its similar makeup could not have been coincidence. Rather, the two passages were clearly composed in relationship to each other. The two passages exhibit a connection that indicates intentionality.

Any clause that reveals parallel material is important for discerning the reason for the intentional connection. These connections exceed mere repetition without purposeful intention. If both passages contain a particular clause, it likely calls attention to this material. This material appears to provide the focus underlying any innertextuality.

The lists of clauses limited to a single passage are likewise important for discerning the strategies and theological intentions imprinted in the composition of the Pentateuch. These clauses should be analyzed for meaningful terms, phrases, or themes. Meaningful terms, phrases, or themes are those items that cohere within the narrative structure of the immediate context, or that cohere within the larger compositional strategies of the Pentateuch. An example of an item that coheres with the immediate context can be seen in Exod 32:8. In that discourse, the Lord reveals the sin of the Israelites to Moses. He also recounts what the people have said about the idol: "These are your gods, Israel, who brought you up from the land of Egypt." Within the context of Exodus 32, this phrase is significant because it repeats verbatim what the Israelites said when the golden calf had been completed.

An example of an item that coheres within the larger compositional strategies within the Pentateuch can be seen in the term כַּעַס "to provoke to anger." This term is used extensively in Deuteronomy 32 and becomes a *leitmotif* in other innertexts.[6] Furthermore, meaningful terms, phrases, or themes limited to a single passage can demonstrate a shifting connotation within the strategy of the composition. These items often exhibit the character of commentary upon those parallel textual units to which they have been innertexted. This aspect of textual commentary by those items limited to a single passage can be detected within the linguistic context in which the parallel material is found.[7] The following verse-by-verse analysis notes any similarities and divergences. Furthermore, it attempts to describe any theological intentions discerned in them.

VERSE-BY-VERSE ANALYSIS

This chapter applies certain criteria of association in order to establish an intentional connection between Exod 32:7–20 and Deut 9:12–21. Once this is accomplished, one is able to adjudicate possible purposes for this connection. This section will use Figure 1 and the catalogue of clauses, phrases, and terminology in order to note any similarities or divergences between the two passages. It will do this in three steps. After noting the similarities and divergences, it will then give the results of the comparison.

First, a lexical comparison will compare the words, phrases, and clauses approximately parallel to one another. This step will note the selection, arrangement, and adaptation of particular textual units. Similarities and divergences will be noted in order to demonstrate the potential for innertextuality and the occasion for it. These similarities and divergences will yield information varying from updated semantic domains to theological intentions.

The second step will analyze textual units on the level of terms, phrases, and clauses limited to one account. This step will note the selec-

---

6. See below, chapter 3. For an analysis of this term and its usage in Deuteronomy and other biblical books, see Joo, *Provocation and Punishment*.

7. Eissfeldt discusses the notion that the poetry of Genesis 49 has repercussions upon those narratives to which it alludes. See Eissfeldt, "kleinste literarische Einheit," 146.

tion, arrangement, adaptation, and writing of particular textual units. It will detect patterns of linguistic elements or themes structurally or compositionally meaningful in those terms, phrases, and clauses limited to one account.

Third, a grammatical and syntactical comparison will be undertaken between those clauses that demonstrate parallel material. Grammatical divergences, such as a change in grammatical person, demonstrate the different narrative contexts from which a clause is drawn. A grammatical similarity could demonstrate the notion of adaptation or writing and also the textual nature of the relationship if used in the parallel passage in a grammatically nonconforming manner. Furthermore, a syntactical comparison will likewise demonstrate similarities and differences between the two accounts, which can then be examined for interpretive value.

These criteria correspond to the first category in Bar-Efrat's article about structural analysis.[8] Structural analysis, in a specific example that Bar-Efrat gives, is "made prominent by means of recurrent words and phrases."[9] Structural analysis provides a correlation to this innertextual analysis between the golden-calf narratives. Bar-Efrat examines a narrative in order to find similar words or phrases that indicate the purposeful structure of a text. This analysis examines similar words, phrases, and clauses between the golden-calf narratives in order to discern innertextuality constituting the compositional strategies within the Pentateuch. Therefore Bar-Efrat's article bears particular importance in discerning this connection.[10]

Lexical Comparison of Parallel Material

This section will compare the words, phrases, and clauses approximately parallel to one another. This will be accomplished by examining those clauses and comparing the lexical stock throughout them. First, parallel material will be noted from the catalogue of clauses and discussed. Second, when the accounts diverge, the difference between the two will be noted and discussed.

8. Bar-Efrat, "Some Observations," 158–70.

9. Ibid., 156.

10. Bar-Efrat discusses three additional levels that can demonstrate narrative structure. These levels could be important for demonstrating textual links among passages if applied to a larger parameter of texts (ibid., 158–70).

PARALLEL MATERIAL BETWEEN EXODUS 32:7-20
AND DEUTERONOMY 9:12-21

The material that corresponds in Exod 32:7-20 and Deut 9:12-21 should express the focus for which the two accounts were linked. These correspondences reflect the motivation for the linkage of these two narratives within the final the shape of the Pentateuch. The parallel clause in Exod 32:7 and Deut 9:12, "And the Lord spoke to ..." initiates the formal correspondence between the two passages. The ensuing parallel clauses clearly emphasize the immediate rebellion of the Israelites in the production of the golden calf. The people whom Moses had brought up from the land of Egypt quickly rebelled against the Lord's command not to make an image. The passages also converge on the notion that Israel is stiff necked. Moreover, although having a distinct emphasis, the passages agree in God's punishment of the people and his making a great nation of Moses. Each of the clauses involved in these correspondences meet criteria of similar terminology, similar syntax, and similar context. Moreover, between these and the ensuing correspondences, the criteria of similar narrative features and a similar sequence of events are met.

Each passage, however, has its own prominence. Additional material in Exodus appears to move the narrative along. The focus of Exodus 32 seems to be on Moses' intercession concerning the Abrahamic covenant and God's restraint from punishing the people. Deuteronomy 9:12-21, although significantly shorter, has its own distinctions. The passages come together again at Moses' descent from the mountain with the tablets. The passages quickly diverge only to correspond again when Moses discovers the idolatrous scene and breaks the tablets. After Moses recounts a prayer, which is limited to Deut 9:18-21a, the two passages agree on Moses' destruction of the calf.

What significance does this material have for an assessment and understanding of the connection between these two passages? First, these terms and motifs conclusively meet the criteria establishing innertextuality. Furthermore, this convergence of material gives prominence to terminology and motifs that run throughout these two passages and any other innertexts within the Pentateuch. These similarities provide the structural focus of the innertextuality. This section has drawn attention to the material that corresponds between the two accounts. The following section will note relatively minor divergences in form between Exod 32:7–20 and Deut 9:12–21.

DIVERGENCES OF LEXEMES IN CLAUSES EXISTING IN EXODUS 32:7–20 AND DEUTERONOMY 9:12–21

This section will note relatively minor divergences in form between the parallel materials. Although divergences occur, this material also meets the criteria of similar terminology, similar syntax, similar narrative features, similar context, and similar sequence of events. Consequently it provides a connection between the two passages and provides a focus for the connection. Exodus 32:7 and Deut 9:12 exhibit the first divergence in the parallel material. Ironically, on the very first occasion of an analogous clause there is a lexical divergence. Exodus 32:7 uses דָּבַר "to speak"; Deut 9:12 has אָמַר "to speak."

The next lexical divergence involves the initial imperatival stem in the ensuing dialogue. Deuteronomy 9:12 uses the verb קוּם ("to arise") while the narrative in Exod 32:7 uses the shortened form of the verb הָלַךְ ("to go"). Aphaereris occurs to shorten the verb to לֵךְ.[11]

The next lexical divergence occurs in the relative clause within the same dialogue. The narrative in Exodus 32 is translated, "whom you brought up from the land of Egypt." The narrative in Deuteronomy 9 is translated, "whom you brought out from Egypt." The difference lies in the verbs underlying an English translation. The book of Exodus uses עָלָה ("to go up") while the narrative in Deuteronomy uses יָצָא ("to go out").

The next lexical divergence is in Exod 32:10 and Deut 9:14. It is a difference involving imperatives. The word הַנִּיחָה, the hiphil imperative of נוח ("to rest"), is used in Exodus 32. The word הֶרֶף, the hiphil imperative of רָפָה ("to sink") is used in Deuteronomy 9.

The next lexical divergence is connected with the two imperatives just discussed. Each of the two imperatives is connected with a prepositional phrase denoting the person with whom the action is connected. The grammatical person in each case is the first-person singular. The prepositions, however, are different. The clause in Exod 32:10 uses the preposition לְ ("to"); the clause in Deut 9:14 uses the preposition מִן ("from").

---

11. Gesenius, et al., *GKC*, 69.

The next lexical divergence involves a verb denoting "to destroy." The narrative in Exodus uses the lexical stem כָּלָה ("to complete"); the narrative in Deuteronomy uses the lexical stem שָׁמַד ("to annihilate").

The next lexical divergence lies at the end of Exod 32:10 and Deut 9:14. Exodus 32:10 says simply, "I will make you into a great nation." Deut 9:14 says, however, "I will make you into a nation more vast and numerous than they." The account in Deuteronomy contains an additional adjective as well as the comparative usage of the adjectives. That divergence suggests a subtle distinction that will be discussed below. Additionally, there is a difference between the adjective directly following the term *nation* in each narrative. Exodus 32:10 uses the term גָּדוֹל ("great"); Deut 9:14 uses the term עָצוּם ("mighty, numerous").

The next lexical divergence occurs in Exod 32:15 and Deut 9:15. In each account the variant term is used in construct with the phrase "and the two tablets." Exod 32:15 uses the term הָעֵדֻת ("testimony"); Deut 9:15 uses the term בְּרִית ("covenant"). The use of this term in Deuteronomy is significant due to the development of the notion of covenant throughout the Pentateuch.

The next lexical divergence concerns the same clause. It is the use of different prepositions. The account in Deuteronomy indicates that the covenant is עַל ("upon, in") the hands of Moses. The account in Exodus, however, uses the inseparable preposition בְּ ("in, with, by").

The next lexical divergence concerns the prepositional phrase indicating where the tablets were broken. The narrative of Exodus 32 states that they were broken תַּחַת הָהָר ("at the base of the mountain"). The account in Deuteronomy 9 indicates that the tablets were broken לְעֵינֵיכֶם ("in front of your eyes").

The next lexical divergence occurs in Exod 32:20 and Deut 9:21. The narrative in Exodus 32 uses the term זָרָה ("to scatter"). In the narrative in Deuteronomy 9, the term שָׁלַךְ ("to throw") is used. Furthermore, this verb in Exod 32:20 has an implied accusative in contrast to Deut 9:21 which has the stated accusative "its dust."

The next divergence involves an entire phrase in which both accounts differ. In Exod 32:20, the phrase "upon the face of the waters" is the place upon which Moses scatters the remains of the calf. Deuteronomy diverges in its use of a preposition as well as in the object of the preposition. The narrative in Deuteronomy uses the preposition אֶל ("to") and the object of the preposition נַחַל ("stream"). In Exod 32:20, the preposition עַל ("upon") is used. Furthermore the account in Exodus 32 uses the noun פָּנִים ("face") in construct with the noun מַיִם ("waters").

This section noted the divergences between the parallel materials. These divergences may show patterns that emerge and indicate coherence with an immediate context or within the compositional strategies of the Pentateuch. These divergences will be examined for consistency with the terms, phrases, and clauses limited to a single passage in order note motifs.

An Analysis of Terms, Phrases, and Clauses Limited to a Single Passage

This section analyzes textual units limited to either Exod 32:7–20 or Deut 9:12–21. In these cases, a term, phrase, or clause is absent in one account but present in the other. The previous comparison of parallel material evinces a correspondence with relatively few divergent lexemes. This analysis, however, will present those elements that are limited to one account. If the congruent elements between the two accounts suggest an intentional connection, this analysis of textual units limited to one account could yield information important for discerning the purpose for the connection. Any noticeable pattern among these textual units should elucidate the reasons for the innertextuality in light of the compositional strategies of the Pentateuch. The section will carry out this comparison by analyzing the dissimilar verbal elements.

DISSIMILAR TEXTUAL UNITS

The first dissimilar unit occurs between Exod 32:7 and Deut 9:12. The phrase מַהֵר מַזֶּה ("quickly from here") occurs in Deut 9:12 but does not occur in the Exodus narrative. This phrase contains an adverb and prepositional phrase. This unit is associated with the preceding imperatives and heightens the intensity of the action in the Deuteronomy account.

The next dissimilar unit is absent in Deut 9:12. In Exod 32:7, the narrative reads, "whom you brought up from the land of Egypt." In Deuteronomy, however, the narrative reads, "whom you brought up from Egypt." The term אֶרֶץ ("land") does not occur in Deut 9:12.

The next dissimilar unit is also not found in Deut 9:12. It is the term עֵגֶל ("calf"). In the narrative of Exodus 32, two terms are used to denote this image: the terms מַסֵּכָה and עֵגֶל ("molten image" and "calf"). In the narrative of Deuteronomy 9, however, only the term מַסֵּכָה ("molten image") is used.

Following the terms עֵגֶל מַסֵּכָה ("molten image calf") in Exod 32:8, a multiclause unit exists that does not occur in Deuteronomy 9. This unit reads, "And they bowed down to it and they sacrificed to it and they said, 'These are your gods, Israel, who brought you up from the land of Egypt.'" This entire unit does not occur in Deuteronomy 9.

The next dissimilar unit occurs between Exod 32:9 and Deut 9:13. In Deut 9:13, the term לֵאמֹר ("saying") is used to introduce the following discourse. This term does not appear in Exod 32:9. Instead the discourse follows the proper name Moses.

Another dissimilar unit occurs between Deut 9:14 and Exod 32:10. In contrast to Deut 9:14, where a unit is absent, Exod 32:10 uses an adverb after the declaration of Israel's character. It is the phrase וְעַתָּה ("and now"). In Deut 9:14, the clause begins with the imperative instead of the waw conjunction and adverb.

A few words later in Deut 9:14, another unit is absent in contrast to Exod 32:10. After the initial imperative in Exod 32:10, the Lord declares, "And my anger will burn against them." This clause does not appear in Deut 9:14. Instead the narrative proceeds directly to the Lord's intention for Israel's destruction.

Following the parallel clause concerning God's destruction of the Israelites, a considerable dissimilar unit occurs between the passages. The narrative in Exod 32:10 does not contain the phrase found in Deuteronomy 9: "And I will wipe out their name from under the heavens."

Another dissimilar unit occurs following that clause. Both accounts contain a clause indicating the Lord's plan to make Moses into a great nation. Although the lexemes are distinct, at least one adjective denotes this greatness. In Deut 9:14, however, another adjective occurs: רַב ("numerous"). Moreover, Deut 9:14 utilizes the comparative adjective מִמֶּנּוּ ("more than") to indicate that Moses will become a more vast and numerous nation than will the Israelites.

The next dissimilar unit involves a large amount of material absent in Deuteronomy 9. It consists of the intercessory prayer and response found in Exod 32:11–14. In the previous verses, a clause was present or absent in the midst of parallel material. By contrast, this section has no parallel material. The corresponding makeup of the material that was encountered in

Exod 32:7–10 and Deut 9:12–14 compels one to ask why this larger block of material is dissimilar between the two accounts.

Exodus 32:11–14 contains material that highlights two matters. The first matter is Moses' intercession for the people. He asks the Lord why his anger burned against his people. He reminds the Lord of what the Egyptians would say. He reminds the Lord of his oath to Abraham, Isaac, and Jacob, his servants, about the multiplying of their descendants, the giving of the land, and their possession of it forever. The second matter is the Lord's repenting over the harm he spoke about doing to his people.

The congruity between the two narratives returns with Exod 32:15 and Deut 9:15. As in the earlier sections of similar material, however, this congruity does not mean exact correspondence. The third clause in Deut 9:15 is absent in Exod 32:15: the phrase "And the mountain was burning with fire."

Shortly after this clause, another dissimilar unit is encountered. This element relates to syntax and deals with the specific number of hands in Deut 9:15: שְׁתֵּי ("two"). In Exod 32:15 the preposition בְּ ("in") is attached directly to the term יַד ("hand").

The next dissimilar unit occurs between Exod 32:19 and Deut 9:16. In the Exod narrative, as Moses draws near to the camp, he sees the calf. The account in Deuteronomy 9, however, contains several units absent in Exodus 32. The first unit is the interjection וְהִנֵּה ("behold"). The second unit consists of the clause "you sinned against the Lord your God." Following this is a recurrent multiclause unit. This multiclause unit already appeared in Deut 9:12. This marks the second time in Deuteronomy 9 that it has been used and attests to the grave nature of the Israelites' sin. It states, "you made for yourselves a calf, a molten image. You turned aside quickly from the way which the Lord your God commanded you." The clause of Exod 32:15 contains the verb רָאָה ("to see") as well as the term עֵגֶל ("calf"), but it does not contain the recurrent clauses.

The next dissimilar unit between Exod 32:19 and Deut 9:16 involves the compound accusative concerning that which Moses saw. In Exod 32:19, he sees the calf and dancing. In Deut 9:16, the dancing is not mentioned; nor is there the clause וַיִּחַר־אַף מֹשֶׁה ("And Moses' anger burned"). Both these units are present in Exod 32:19 but absent in Deut 9:16.

The next dissimilar unit concerns a phrase in Deut 9:19 that is not in Exod 32:19. The first-person description of Moses' action, "And I took hold of the two tablets," follows the account of Moses' action upon his seeing the molten calf. Exodus 32:19 presumes that the tablets are already in Moses' hands.

In the description of the location of the tablets in Deut 9:17, the account in Deuteronomy 9 again specifies that Moses cast them מֵעַל שְׁתֵּי יָדָי ("from upon the two of my hands"). The two tablets are indicated by the third person plural pronoun ם ("them"). The Exodus account simply uses an inseparable preposition with the noun ("from his hands").

Whereas the account in Deuteronomy used a third-person personal pronoun to identify the tablets, the account in Exodus did not. Consequently, Exod 32:19 must now state the accusative אֶת־הַלֻּחֹת ("the tablets"). Deuteronomy 9:17 has no need to do this, as it had already identified the object of casting with the pronoun.

In Deut 9:18, the author records Moses' second stay of forty days and nights on the mountain. Peculiarly, this account seems to correspond to Exod 34:4–28.[12] Here in Deuteronomy 9, the first-person narrative records Moses' intercession and fasting about the sin and evil the Israelites did in order to provoke the Lord. The dissimilar unit continues, relating Moses' fear for the people in light of God's anger and rage—enough to destroy them. The Lord listened and did not destroy the people or Aaron, although he was angry enough with Aaron to destroy him. Even though it is possible that this material refers to the intercession in Exodus 34, the material itself is distinct in many cases. Except for the reference to the forty days and forty nights, no other similar clauses exist between Deut 9:18–20 and Exod 34:4–28. It is more likely that Deut 9:18–20 refers to Exod 32:30–35. Regardless, its presence here indicates the seriousness of the sin of the golden calf. The recurring nominal and verbal forms of the term חָטָא ("sin") signal a motif in the Deuteronomic account. Moreover, the term כָּעַס ("to provoke to anger") links this passage with other inner-texts important within the book of Deuteronomy (Deut 4:25, 31:29, 32:16, 19, 21, and 27) and the Pentateuch.

Exod 32:20 and Deut 9:21 once again display marked similarities. The two verses are, however, syntactically distinct and contain dissimilar textual units, which must be noted. First, Exod 32:20 states that Moses took the calf that they made. The statement in Deut 9:21, however, in-

---

12. Driver, *Deuteronomy*, 114–15. The purpose and understanding of Moses' multiple extended mountain intercessions in the book of Deuteronomy lies outside the scope of this analysis. For a recent analysis of the entire episode, see Talstra, "Deuteronomy 9 and 10," 187–210.

dicates not only the accusative "calf" but also the accusative וְאֶת־חַטַּאתְכֶם ("your sin")

The next dissimilar unit involves the distinct verb כָּתַת ("to beat") in Deut 9:21. After Moses burns the calf, he then beats it before grinding it thoroughly. In Exod 32:20, Moses burns the calf and proceeds to grind it without any mention of the verb "to beat."

The next dissimilar unit concerns the extent to which Moses ground the burnt idol. In Exod 32:20, Moses grinds it until it was crushed. In the corresponding account in Deut 9:21, Moses beats it, grinding it thoroughly, until it was crushed. The term הֵיטֵב ("thoroughly") is not used in the Exodus account.

Again in Deut 9:21, another distinct unit indicates the extent to which the idol is pulverized. Exodus 32:20 and Deut 9:21 both state that Moses ground the calf until it was crushed. Both narratives proceed to record the tossing of the substance upon water. In the Deuteronomic account, however, the term לְעָפָר ("to dust") is used to denote the extent to which the object was ground.

The next dissimilar unit once again involves the term עָפָר ("dust") In Deut 9:21, it serves as the direct object. The term עָפָר ("dust") receives the action of the verb "cast." These elements are not found in Exod 32:20, where the implied direct object of the clause "and he tossed" is the term "calf." This implied direct object is held over from the initial clause in Exod 32:20.

The final dissimilar unit between Exod 32:20 and Deut 9:21 involves the remains of the calf after it has been scattered over the water. In Exod 32:20, וַיַּשְׁקְ אֶת־בְּנֵי יִשְׂרָאֵל׃ ("Moses gave it to the sons of Israel to drink"). This final clause is absent in Deut 9:21. In the narrative from Deuteronomy, the final glimpse of the remains of the idol is depicted as flowing down the mountain.

The remaining material in Exodus 32 and Deuteronomy 9 is dissimilar. In Deuteronomy 9 Moses turns to the rebellions of Israel at Taberah, Massah, and Kibroth-Hattaavah, where they had provoked the Lord. He also speaks of the time when the Lord sent them from Kadesh-Barnea in order that they could possess the land he had given them, but they would not believe the Lord or listen to the Lord's voice. Moses reiterates Israel's rebelliousness for as long as he (Moses) [had known them. Furthermore, Moses reminds the people that he himself had interceded for them so that the Lord would not destroy them. The account in Exodus 32 portrays the aftermath of the incident of idolatry. Moses questions Aaron, and the Lord punishes the Israelites by the swords of Moses and the Levites.

This section noted those textual units limited to a single account and began to discern the importance of certain terms, phrases, or themes. The next section registers the grammatical and syntactical entries which are distinct and draws out the importance of particular emphases.

Grammatical-Syntactical Comparison

This comparison will register those grammatical and syntactical entries that are distinct. In order for this to be accomplished, the entries of Exod 32:7–20 between Deut 9:12–21 must run parallel. A notation will be made where parallel clauses between the two accounts approximately but not precisely conform to each other in lexeme and verbal content. As previously stated, if the preponderance of parallel material between the two accounts shows that Exod 32:7–20 and Deut 9:12–21 were written in relationship to each other, any similarities or departures call for interpretive reflection. Similar forms demonstrate the connection and provide the focus of it. Distinct forms likely suggest an underlying reason for their use.

Distinct Grammatical and Syntactical Forms

The first distinct form in Exod 32:7–35 in contrast with Deut 9:12–29 can be found in the initial verses of the comparison. As will be noted throughout, a major grammatical difference results from the different narrative viewpoints. The narratives in Exodus are written from a third-person perspective. The Lord is speaking to Moses. Any first-person perspective is written within discourse framed by the third person narrative account. Although Deuteronomy is also framed by an overall narrative framework, it is largely portrayed as a first-person explanation of the law in Deut 1:5: בְּאֵר אֶת־הַתּוֹרָה ("to explain the law"). In the Deuteronomy narrative, the character, Moses, tells the story from his own viewpoint. Consequently, the grammatical first person is used. Many first person verbs in Deuteronomy are distinct from their third person counterparts in Exodus. These distinct forms occur between Exod 32:7a and Deut 9:12a and between Exod 32:9a and Deut 9:13a.

Distinct syntactical forms are present in Exod 32:10a and Deut 9:14a. In the former, a *waw + x + qetol* clause is present whereas in the latter a *qetol* form begins the clause.[13] Furthermore, this phrase in Exodus contains an inseparable preposition with a first-person suffix. Alternately, the phrase in Deuteronomy contains an inseparable preposition with another form of the first-person pronoun.[14]

Another distinct form occurs between Exod 32:15a–b and Deut 9:15a–b. This difference involves a change in grammatical person. In Exodus, the narrator spoke of Moses in the third person. In the account in Deuteronomy, Moses is portrayed as speaking, and the material is thus in the first person. Therefore a first-person personal pronoun is used instead of the proper name Moses.

More distinct forms occur between Exod 32:15c and Deut 9:15d due to the absence or presence of a preposition. In Exod 32:15c, the tablets of the testimony are בְ ("in his hand"). In the account in Deut 9:15d, the two tablets of the covenant are עַל ("upon the two of my hands").

Distinct forms occur in Exod 32:19b and Deut 9:16a. This difference involves a change in grammatical person. Furthermore a distinct form is used in Exod 32:19b, in which Moses sees the calf. The direct object marker אֵת is used to indicate the accusative noun "calf." The clause in Deuteronomy, however, contains no such direct-object marker. Rather, textual units are repeated that call attention to the sin of the Israelites in making the calf.

The subsequent distinct forms occur between Exod 32:19d and Deut 9:17b. This difference again involves a change in grammatical person. Moreover, in Exodus, the direct-object marker indicates the object of the verb "to cast." In Deut 9:17b, the direct object is the third-person plural form attached to the verb. Its antecedent, "the two tablets," is carried over from the previous clause. Furthermore another distinct form occurs concerning the description of the tablets in Moses' hands. In Exodus the tablets are cast "from his hands." In Deuteronomy, the tablets are cast "from upon the two of my hands."

The distinct forms forming Exod 32:20 and Deut 9:21 are the most syntactically diverse clauses between the parallel materials. Exodus 32:20 begins with a *wayyiqtol* verbal form. This type of verbal form foregrounds the action of the narrative.[15] This form is distinct from the parallel account

13. The *waw* is the conjunction; the *x* indicates that a form is in a position prior to the verb; *qetol* indicates and imperative form.

14. Gesenius, et al., *GKC*, 302–3.

15. Schneider, *Grammatik des biblischen Hebräisch*, 177–78.

in Deuteronomy in part due to the different perspective in grammatical person, which has now recurred frequently between the parallel passages. Furthermore, the verb in Exod 32:20a is completed by the direct-object marker with the accusative definite noun אֶת־הָעֵגֶל ("the calf"). In Deut 9:21, however, the corresponding verb appears in fourth position instead of beginning the sentence. It is important to note at this juncture that the exact same lexemes are used in both Exodus and Deuteronomy, except for the first noun phrase in Deut 9:21. Rather than with a *waw* consecutive carrying the narrative forward, Deut 9:21 begins with a direct-object marker and a noun phrase: וְאֶת־חַטַּאתְכֶם ("your sin"). Such an obvious disruption of normal syntax is likely to be significant since the practice of retaining typical Hebrew syntax has consistently been demonstrated throughout the account. Moreover, the fact that the same lexemes were available but not used in the same order suggests a purpose for the distinct usage. This occurrence of nonconforming syntax and nonconforming lexical usage meets the criterion of a break in a recognizable textual unit and the criterion of contextual awareness. The presence of the additional noun phrase suggests a new formulation in order to provide an emphasis. These factors convincingly demonstrate the intentional and meaningful connection between the two passages.[16]

Although it was noted above, the beginning noun phrase וְאֶת־חַטַּאתְכֶם ("your sin") was absent in Exod 32:20. It seems to correspond to the direct-object marker and accusative noun אֶת־הָעֵגֶל ("the calf"), which is present in both accounts. Its initial position and distinct occurrence suggest that the sin of the Israelites in the production of the golden calf remains the central focus of the narrative in Deuteronomy 9.

The next distinct forms again involve Exod 32:20 and Deut 9:21. In Exod 32:20, the term אֶת־הָעֵגֶל ("the calf") is in second position. It immediately follows the verb לקח. In the parallel account in Deut 9:21, the noun phrase אֶת־הָעֵגֶל ("the calf") no longer follows the verb, "to take." Instead it occurs immediately before this verb and follows the relative clause אֲשֶׁר־עֲשִׂיתֶם ("which you made"). The parallel clause in Exod 32:20,

---

16. The disruption of typical narrative syntax normally carried forward by the *wayyiqtol*, and that syntax that occurs in the parallel material of Exod 32:20, suggest a more likely scenario that Deuteronomy is dependent on the account in Exodus rather than that Exod 32:20 alludes to Deut 9:21. For a discussion of the direction of dependence, see Begg, "Destruction of the Calf"; Begg, "Destruction of the Golden Calf Revisited"; Schmitt, "Die Erzählung vom Goldenen Kalb," 235–50; and Hayes, "Golden Calf Stories." Cf. Van Seters, *Life of Moses*, 290–318.

אֲשֶׁר עָשׂוּ ("which they made"), occurs immediately after the phrase אֶת־הָעֵגֶל ("the calf"). Deuteronomy 9:21a effectually highlights the objects "calf" and "sin" and the verb "to make." In Exodus 32, Moses' action of taking the calf is connoted in normal narrative syntax.[17]

Another distinction in syntax between the two accounts again involves the grammatical person of the verb שׂרף ("to burn") in Exod 32:20b and Deut 9:21b. Furthermore a distinct form occurs, involving the absence of the direct-object marker and the pronominal suffix in Exod 32:20b. The following clause in Exod 32:20c consists of a *wayyiqtol* verb with a prepositional phrase: וַיִּטְחַן עַד אֲשֶׁר־דָּק ("And he ground [it] until it was crushed"). In the corresponding clause in Deut 9:21c, the same four lexical roots occur with an additional term: הֵיטֵב ("thoroughly"). However, the lexeme that occurred as a *wayyiqtol* in Exodus 32 is an infinitive absolute in Deuteronomy: טָחוֹן ("grinding").

RESULTS OF THE COMPARISON

The previous analysis shows distinctions between the two parallel accounts. In spite of these, the formal similarities in terminology, phrases, clauses, and content demonstrate the connection between Exod 32:7–20 and Deut 9:12–21. Figure 1 and the catalogue of clauses, phrases, and terminology show congruent elements between the two passages. This congruency goes beyond coincidence to make evident an intentional connection between the two passages.

Questions about the intention for the similarities and divergences remain. The parallel material provides the focus for the connection. The divergences provide a further basis for discerning theological intentions between these and any other innertexts. Chapter 3 briefly applies criteria of association to other passages within the Pentateuch that show signs of innertextuality. Within the final shape of the Pentateuch, these innertexts fold back upon and interpret the connected passages. By means of such connected passages, the compositional strategies are made evident.

Another significant factor in understanding these texts involves the programmatic statement reflected in Deut 1:5. Israel is finally ready to enter the Promised Land. Deuteronomy 1:5 indicates that as Israel stood on the banks of the Jordan, prepared to cross into the land, Moses explained the Torah. This programmatic statement and what follows it

17. Schneider, *Grammatik des biblischen Hebräisch*, 178–80.

has implications for the entire Pentateuch. Moses' "explanation" includes more than legal material only. Immediately following Deut 1:5, Moses' explanation deals with the time the people departed from Mount Sinai. Moses is portrayed as explaining the narrative material within the Torah. Deuteronomy 9 is likewise such an explanation of narrative material. This structural framework given in Deut 1:5 proposes an interpretive function to the book of Deuteronomy.

This interpretive function is precisely what is seen in Deut 9:12–21. The criteria demonstrate the intentional connection between Exod 32:7–20 and Deut 9:12–21. The connections show that the author is interpreting what is *written* in Exodus 32. Within the book of Deuteronomy and the compositional strategies of the Pentateuch an obvious interpretive function is at work. The focus is not an interpretation of law codes or a recapitulation of a bare event. The similarities suggest that every textual unit within the composition has a purpose. The following section will use the interpretive factor in the book of Deuteronomy along with implications brought about by the intentional connection between the two passages in order to explain the similarities and differences.

Interpreting the Similarities and Divergences

The above analysis registers every divergence between the passages. Some differences involve significant numbers of lexemes and clauses. Others consist of grammatical and stylistic issues. The following remarks based on the comparison above deal with those factors which are judged to be significant within the compositional strategies of the Pentateuch.

An additional phrase indicates a distinction shortly after the parallel material begins in Exod 32:7 and Deut 9:12. In the initial verses of Deuteronomy 9, Moses reminded the people of their provocation of the Lord. At Horeb, God had commanded them from the midst of the fire, and Moses was given the tablets. After the forty-day session on the mountain, the Lord compelled Moses not only to go down as in the account in Exodus 32 but to go down "quickly from this place." These words are absent in the Exodus account.

The fact that this is present in Deuteronomy lends a particular urgency to the situation. The adverb indicates a sense of urgency: the Israelites have acted ruinously and peril is certain. Furthermore, the demonstrative pronoun "this place" prompts the reader to consider what was taking place when the Lord spoke. Moses was on top of the mountain receiving the very words that forbade such an action. This again assists the reader in detecting the weight of the Israelites' action.

The remainder of Deut 9:12 demonstrates the analogous makeup of the two accounts. Although lexical differences do occur, it appears that a parallel text is available. The precise phraseology and syntax illustrate this point. This precise makeup of the connection provides the focus of the connection: "your people acted corruptly whom you brought out of Egypt." The similarity should not be lost on the reader. The composer shows his willingness to arrange and adapt the textual units at different points between the passages. Here though the exact terminology is maintained between the two passages except for one word: אֶרֶץ ("land"). The parallel material calls attention to the action of the Israelites. No sooner did the Lord command them than they were breaking his command. When looked at in the context of Deuteronomy 9, this is consistent with what Moses is portraying. Moses speaks a similar notion in Deut 9:7 when he says, "Since the day when you went out from the land of Egypt until you came to this place, you have been rebelling against the Lord."

Another divergence takes place at the end of Deut 9:12. The clause reads "they turned quickly aside from the way which I commanded them; they made for themselves a molten image." In Exod 32:8, two terms are used: "calf" and "molten image." The term עֵגֶל ("calf") is used eleven times in the Pentateuch.[18] In Lev 9:2, 3, and 8, the term is used in reference to the sacrificial system. The remaining instances connote the idol that Aaron had made. In the portrayal in Deuteronomy, the term מַסֵּכָה is used, which denotes a molten image set up for the purpose of idolatry. The eight occurrences of this term in the Pentateuch denote idolatry through some molten image. The collocation "a calf, a molten image" appears in Deut 9:16 in precisely the same form as that found in Exod 32:8. This suggests that it was available to use. The absence here of the term "calf" possibly hints that a more general practice of idolatry is in view in the midst of this narrative. It is not only this specific occasion of worshiping the golden calf; rather, a wider range of idolatry comes into view and is considered direct disobedience against the first and oft-given commandment prohibiting idolatry.[19]

---

18. Even-Shoshan, *New Concordance of the Bible*, 829.

19. Exod 20:3, 23, 34:17; Lev 19:4, 26:1; Deut 4:16, 23, 25, 5:8, 27:15.

The next significant distinction occurs in the ensuing clause of Exod 32:8. The Exodus account has four clauses that do not occur in Deuteronomy. What is the explanation for this? Is this evidence that Exodus and Deuteronomy each come from a distinct source? It appears evident from the similar terms, phrases, and clauses from Exod 32:7-8b and Deut 9:12 that the two passages are intentionally associated. Furthermore Deuteronomy is purported to be Moses' explanation of the law (Deut 1:5). In light of these factors, what would be the purpose of this absence of otherwise analogous material between these two passages? It appears that the book of Deuteronomy is not concerned to relate the clauses "and they bowed down to it, and they sacrificed to it, and they said, 'These are your Gods, Israel, who brought you up from the land of Egypt.'"

It is not immediately clear why this clause is absent. The effect, however, has two results. First, it reveals that it was sufficient that the Israelites made the calf. They did not need to bow down to it, sacrifice to it, and declare it to have redeemed them in order to provoke the Lord. Second, without these clauses, the author is able to move directly to the outcome of the idol production. The outcome is stated in both texts and seems to be an emphasis within the strategy of Deuteronomy 9: The people are stiff necked. The two statements are identical. That this statement occurs in the Deuteronomy account is consistent within the structure of the book of Deuteronomy. The people have been in rebellion against the Lord and have refused to trust him (Deut 1:32, 43).

This intentional association of these two passages can be seen in this description of the Israelites. The author of Deuteronomy is taking the incident of the golden calf and using it as an example to typify the character of the Israelites throughout the Pentateuch. Moses warns the people in the opening verses of Deuteronomy 9: It is not because of their righteousness that the Lord is giving them the land. Before repeating the lesson of the golden calf, Moses himself calls the people stiff necked in Deuteronomy 9:6. His use of this description before the account of the golden calf reveals his purpose for including this description ("stiff necked"). He wants to use the incident to typify the character of the Israelites from the beginning, even after the Lord's deliverance of them from Egypt.

The next distinction likewise uncovers a purpose in the connection between Exod 32:7-20 and Deut 9:12-21. In Exodus 32 after describing the Israelites as stiff necked, the Lord continues, "And now, leave me and let my anger burn against them and I will finish them and I will make you into a great nation" (v. 10). The corresponding statement in Deuteronomy is similar enough to show a connection but different enough to be significant. An adverbial phrase begins the Exod 32:10. After a parallel command to be left alone, Exodus 32 records the anger of the Lord. The Lord would naturally be angry after such disobedience and would subsequently אֲכַלֵּם ("bring them to an end"). After that, he would then make Moses into a great nation.

The account in Deuteronomy, however, is different. First, there is no adverb to commence Deut 9:14. Moreover, there is no description of the Lord's anger. This absence achieves a particular terseness in Deut 9:14. It is abrupt, and the following verbs add to the severity of the effect. Instead of bringing them to an end, the Lord would אַשְׁמִידֵם ("destroy them"). In addition, he would wipe their name from under heaven. The use of this verb ("wipe out") signals a grave posture against the Israelites. This verb מָחָה ("to wipe out") is used in pentateuchal contexts that serve as a strong judgment against the offending party.[20] Moreover, the exact phrase אֶת־שְׁמָם מִתַּחַת הַשָּׁמָיִם "their name from under the heavens" occurs in Deut 7:24. This verse says that the Lord would deliver the kings of the enemy into their hands, and that they would cause them to perish "from under the heavens." Such an exact phrase shows not only an association between these two passages but a reversal of what was supposed to happen. Other names were to be eradicated from under heaven. But here God threatens to do the same to Israel. From the retrospective view of Deuteronomy, the golden-calf incident is indicative not only of God's past relationship to Israel; it is determinative for the future. The author of Deuteronomy intimates a questionable future for the people.

The next parallel clause displays a periodic theme within the Pentateuch. God is not dependent on the Israelites to accomplish his purposes. Both accounts state that God will use Moses to make the nation that he so desires. Deuteronomy contains the additional adjectives: עָצוּם ("vast") instead of גָּדוֹל ("great"), another adjective רָב ("numerous"), and the comparative usage of both adjectives. Similar phrases are found in Exod 1:9 and Num 22:6 within contexts that indicate God's blessing on the numerous Israelites. This seems to suggest that God will bless Moses and make him into a greater nation than Israel. Again it appears that the future of the people is uncertain.

20. Gen 6:7, 7:4, 23; Exod 17:14, 32, 33; Deut 25:19, 29:19.

This account shows signs of being composed from other small units of text. In addition to those mentioned above, this clause ("and I will make you into a mightier and greater nation than they") approximately agrees with Num 14:12. In that passage, a similar situation is taking place. The people have provoked the Lord, and he threatens to destroy them and make Moses into a great nation. The compositional makeup demonstrates the selection of these small units found in other portions of the Pentateuch.

The next section, in Exod 32:11-14, is absent in Deuteronomy 9. As stated above in the analysis, the section comprises Moses' intercession and the Lord's subsequent action. The fact that it is absent at this juncture in Deuteronomy 9 intimates that this author is not concerned yet to portray Moses as intercessor or to show that the Lord has relented of the calamity he would send. Once again, from the situation prescribed in Deut 1:5, it appears that this is intentional as the composer moves to select, arrange, and adapt the text in order to communicate his meaning. If this is the case, what would be the significance of this absence? It seems that the author is not ready to portray this act of intercession, the content of the intercession, or the outcome of the intercession. Moses does intercede for the Israelites in Deut 9:18-20. The result is much more uncertain than in Exodus, however, and will be commented on below. As for the absence at this point in Deuteronomy 9, the author is not ready to say that the Lord repented of sending calamity.

The content of the intercession in Exodus is also significant. That content includes the oath made to Abraham, Isaac, and Israel concerning their multiplied seed. It further includes the unit וְכָל־הָאָרֶץ הַזֹּאת אֲשֶׁר אָמַרְתִּי אֶתֵּן לְזַרְעֲכֶם ("and all this land which I said I will give to your seed"). This unit approximately agrees with the land declaration found in Gen 12:7, 24:7, and 26:3. The nearly verbatim use of this declaration in Exodus 32 shows the compositional makeup of Exodus. The absence of this in Deuteronomy is best explained as an intentional exclusion of this particular unit. This absence implies that the land promise is not the focus in Deuteronomy 9. The issue of the acquisition of land remains important but conspicuously absent at this juncture. Likewise, the absence of the clause "and they will possess [it] forever" raises the question of its relevance. This statement remains in question because of the rebellion of the Israelites.

In both accounts Moses is now seen as turning and heading down the mountain. In Deuteronomy, however, the mountain is burning with fire. It is the presence of this phrase that intensifies the scene in Deuteronomy. This phrase is reminiscent of the scene in Exodus 19 at Mount Sinai. Deuteronomy 4:11 and 5:23 are in view, where the precise phrase וְהָהָר בֹּעֵר בָּאֵשׁ ("and the mountain was burning with fire") is used. The contexts of Deut 4:11 and 5:23 both involve the giving of the law on Mount Sinai. The inclusion of this phrase at this juncture associates this portrayal with those passages. The giving of the law was a most serious occasion. Likewise was Israel's disobedience of that same law.[21]

Another difference often pointed out involves the different noun in construct with the tablets. In Exod 32:15, the term עֵדֻת ("testimony") is used. In the corresponding verse in Deut 9:15, the term בְּרִית ("covenant") is used. The term "covenant" is used in connection with the lawgiving at Sinai on repeated occasions in Deuteronomy. Deuteronomy 4:13, 23, 5:2, 3, 9:9, 11, and 15 make reference to the covenant given at Sinai. This reference is no different, and it highlights the connection between the giving of the law at Sinai and the breaking of the covenant.

In Exod 32:15d–19a, there is again the absence of material in Deuteronomy compared with Exodus. The Exodus material can be broken down into two topics. The first topic is the tablets and what was inscribed on them. A rather lengthy and repetitive statement is made about the nature of the tablets: They were written on both sides, they were the work of God, and God himself engraved the writing upon the tablets. The syntax of this material is not written along the main line of the narrative.[22] The lack of *wayyiqtol* forms indicates the makeup of this material. It likely gives circumstantial information about God's involvement in the production of the tablets.[23] The second topic deals with the short narrative in which Joshua hears noise in the camp. Moses responds in elevated fashion.

The makeup of the clauses about the tablets in Exod 32:15–16 appears syntactically peculiar. After the initial verbs of Exod 32:15, no verbal forms appear throughout Exod 32:16. Consequently there are no *wayyiqtol* forms to carry the narrative. As stated, these clauses appear to

---

21. Biddle, *Deuteronomy*, 165.

22. Schneider, *Grammatik des biblischen Hebräisch*, 178.

23. Ibid., 178–80.

highlight the divine origin of the tablets before Moses destroys them. The reason for the absence of these clauses from Deuteronomy 9 is not immediately clear. The discussion between Joshua and Moses about noise in the camp does pick up the narrative sequence in Exod 32:17. The reason for its absence in Deuteronomy is likewise not immediately transparent. The initial verb of Deut 9:16 does correspond to the verb in Exod 32:19b, although the grammatical person is different. Furthermore, in Exod 32:19b the accusative immediately follows the verb, in typical Hebrew style.[24] Such is not the case in Deut 9:16.

In Deut 9:16, after the first-person *waw* consecutive verb וָאֵרֶא ("to see"), the narrative chain ceases, and the subject of the sin of the golden calf is again made the point. The analogous material between Exod 32:7-10, 15a-b, 19, 20 and Deut 9:12-14, 15a-b, 16-17, 21 demonstrates that the narratives were composed in connection with each other. In light of these connections, a reason for the absence of the aforementioned material from Deuteronomy 9 can now be proposed: The material about the writing on the tablets and the narrative about noise in the camp appear to be absent in Deuteronomy in order to prolong the spotlight on the sin of the golden calf. In Deuteronomy, the focus is neither on the content of the tablets nor on the discovery of the situation at the camp.

The focus rather is on the subsequent three clauses. Two of these clauses occur earlier in this same narrative (Deut 9:12). Deuteronomy 9:16-17 says, "And behold, you sinned against the Lord. You made for yourselves a molten calf. You turned aside quickly from the way which the Lord commanded you." Aside from grammatical person and an additional term denoting the calf, these two clauses are identical to the clauses in Deut 9:12. One should presume from the absence of material related to the tablets in Deuteronomy and these repeated clauses that the focus is on the sin of the Israelites in the production of the golden calf. The approximately verbatim repetition of these clauses conclusively draws attention to the importance of this material within Deuteronomy 9 as well as other innertextual passages.

The final two clauses of Exod 32:19 and the parallel material of Deut 9:17 converge on the shattering of the tablets. The use of these two clauses in both accounts serves to reinforce the result of the sin. In anger, Moses shatters the tablets. The anger of Moses in Exod 32:19 rightly perplexes

---

24. Pratico and Van Pelt, *Basics of Biblical Hebrew Grammar*, 276.

scholars.[25] Why would Moses be angry since the Lord had already warned him? The issue could be sidestepped if a harmonization was our purpose. That objective would not answer the question, however, of why either account is arranged in this manner. Furthermore, it would not provide the reason for the connection between the two passages. The clause that relates Moses' anger is absent in the Deuteronomic account. The passages converge at the point that connects the sin of the golden calf to the giving of the law. The tablets are a reminder of what happened on Mount Sinai. Not unlike the mountain burning with fire, the intentional association of the two accounts at this point focuses the issue again on this momentous occasion of the giving of the law. Israel's idolatry compels Moses to shatter the commandments.

The account in Deuteronomy does prolong this scene. Both passages contain a clause indicating that Moses threw the tablets from his hand. In Deut 9:17a, however, the narrative devotes an additional clause to the moment.[26] Moses says, "And I laid hold of the two of the tablets." Furthermore, in Exod 32:19, the tablets are broken at the bottom of the mountain. The accounts diverge at this point. The account in Deut 9:17 draws attention to the personal nature of what had transpired. It reads, "And I broke them before your eyes." Because the prolonged view of the scene and the eyewitness view are absent in Exod 32:19, Deuteronomy appears to focus on the effect that the idolatry has on the covenant. It is shattered before the people's very eyes.

At this juncture Deuteronomy 9 has material not parallel to Exodus 32. The material from Deut 9:18–20 contains Moses' intercession on behalf of the people and Aaron. Strangely, this occasion is possibly the second occasion of Moses' return to the top of the mountain, narrated in Exodus 34. In the Exodus account, Moses undertakes the burning and grinding of the calf before this. Consequently, the arrangement of the units in their respective contexts diverges. What would be the purpose of this arrangement? In Deuteronomy, the intercession appears to cover more than the immediate sin of the golden calf. That specific incident of idolatry is still in view due to the return of that subject in the narrative at Deut 9:21. However, the fact that Moses fell before the Lord and fasted "concerning all your sin which you sinned to do evil in the eyes of the Lord in order

25. Childs, *Book of Exodus*, 558; Schmitt, "Die Erzählung vom Goldenen Kalb," 237–38.

26. Bar-Efrat, *Narrative Art in the Bible*, 141–50.

to provoke him" indicates a pattern of behavior. It is not so much that the incident of the golden calf is not in view, but rather that there is a larger purpose in mind. The words "all your sin" in Deut 9:21 suggest more than just this occasion. Moreover, the Lord was angry enough with Aaron to destroy him. This is the same term that is used against the Israelites in Deut 9:14 when God threatens to "destroy them," "wipe out their name from under heaven," and "make [Moses] into a greater nation." Also absent is any mention of the Abrahamic covenant and God's decision not to do harm to the Israelites. The absence of these units suggests that God's hand of punishment is not necessarily stayed.

Moreover, the narrative in Deuteronomy 9 appears to be dealing with a larger pattern of rebellion. Besides the repetition of terms "sin," "stiff-necked," and "to provoke to anger," another indicator that a pattern of rebellion remains in view is the repeated occurrences of the forty-day-and-night fast. This pattern can be seen in Deut 9:18, 25 and 10:10 for the same purpose of staying the Lord's destruction of the people. A third indicator that this is a pattern is seen by the series of events that follow Deut 9:21. Deuteronomy 9:22–24 says, "And at Taberah and at Massah and at Kibroth-hattaavah you were provoking the Lord to anger. And when the Lord sent you from Kadesh-barnea, saying, 'Go up and possess the land which I have given you,' and you rebelled against the command of the Lord your God and you neither believed in him nor listened to his voice. You have been rebelling against the Lord from the day I knew you." It is clear that this section of Deuteronomy 9 is establishing a larger pattern that shows the Israelites' inability to follow the Lord. Instead they provoke him and are stiff-necked.

At this point in Deuteronomy 9, the future of the Israelites seems unclear. No mention has been made that the Lord has repented of either doing harm to his people or replacing them with a nation from Moses. As mentioned in the analysis above, the correspondence between Exod 32:20 and Deut 9:21 converges in lexical choice but diverges in syntax. The resulting text suggests that the precise correspondence between the two accounts could have been retained. The difference in word order and the additional accusative leaves little doubt where the emphasis lies. "Your sin, which you made, the golden calf I took and I burned . . ." The composition of Deuteronomy 9 unambiguously emphasizes the archetypal sin of the golden calf. At every turn in the narrative, the portrayal of the Israelites displays a people bent on rebellion.

Moreover, the attention exhibited in Deut 9:21 by the additional verb "to beat," the additional adverb, "thoroughly," and the resulting noun phrase, "to dust," shows the intensity in which the Deuteronomic account illustrates the destruction of the object of idolatry. Certainly the narrative in Deuteronomy 9 typified the golden calf as the sin which epitomized the rebelliousness of the Israelite nation.

The ensuing verse, Deut 9:22, offers an important comment about the Israelites. It states, "And at Taberah and at Massah and at Kibroth-hattaavah you were provoking the Lord to anger." These are all instances within the Pentateuch where the Israelites had provoked the Lord.[27]

This section attempted to discern the theological intentions for the similarities and divergences between Exod 32:7–20 and Deut 9:12–21. Moreover, this chapter has established that a comparison of these two passages conclusively meets the criteria of similar terminology, similar syntax, and similar context. Moreover, the chapter has established the relationship between the passages met the criteria of a similar sequence of events, contextual awareness, and the breaking of a pattern. By noting these criteria in the Exodus and Deuteronomy accounts, this chapter demonstrated the intentional connection between Exod 32:7–20 and Deut 9:12–21. Furthermore, this chapter utilized the intentional connections to adjudicate the focus of those connections and the possible reasons for the divergences within the contexts of the two passages.

---

27. Sailhamer, *Pentateuch as Narrative*, 443.

3

The Innertextuality of Exodus 32:7–20 and Deuteronomy 9:12–21 and the Structure of the Pentateuch

B Y DEFINITION, INNERTEXTUALITY RELATES to the entirety of a work. The linguistic connections that make up innertextuality should be distributed in some manner over the entirety of a text. If the linguistic connections that exist in a work are not distributed throughout the work, it likely falls short of innertextuality. Innertextuality serves to unite a work and to provide a framework for discerning a strategy within a composition. According to Fohrer, a feature that makes composition distinct from redaction is the compositional notations that are distributed throughout the document and relate to its entirety. These notations are not limited to an immediate context; nor do they serve in a manner of mere bridging.[1] Instead, the notations serve to unite the work and demonstrate thematic purposes within a text. In this way, innertextuality should be seen throughout a completed text. Innertextuality is most obvious when numerous instances of linguistic connections are recognized throughout the work.

The task remains to examine the rest of the Pentateuch for innertextuality among texts related to Exod 32:7–20 and Deut 9:12–21. This chapter will use the criteria established in chapter 1 in order to identify other innertextual passages within the Pentateuch. The criteria of similar terminology and similar context will make up the majority of these connections. These passages will substantiate the importance of the theme of idolatry within the Pentateuch. The purpose of this chapter is to suggest other passages within the Pentateuch that demonstrate an innertextual likeness to Exod 32:7–20 and Deut 9:12–21.

1. Fohrer, *Exegese des Alten Testaments*, 143–47.

DEUTERONOMY 32:16–21

Deut 32:17 has strong innertextual connections to Exod 32:7–20 and Deut 9:12–21. First, a context of idolatry can be found in Deut 32:16: "They made him jealous with foreign ones." The Hebrew verb קָנָא ("made him jealous") is the verbal parallel to the adjective קַנָּה ("jealous") found in many idolatry passages. Deuteronomy 32:21 utilizes the same verbal form as Deut 32:16, denoting Israel's propensity to make God jealous with other gods. This word used three times in this passage occurs in each of the four contexts concerning the Ten Commandments, which begin, of course, with a prohibition of idolatry. The prohibition of idolatry in Exod 20:1–5; 34:14; and Deut 4:24; 5:9; and 6:15 refer to the Lord as jealous for his people's devotion in relationship to deities or idols. In the seven occurrences of this root in the book of Deuteronomy, it is used in the context of God's being jealous for his people as they abandon him for other gods.

After the initial verb in Deut 32:16, one finds that they made God jealous with "strange gods."[2] This term refers to foreign gods that were not related to Israel's covenant-making God, Yahweh. God consistently warned Israel not to play the harlot with the gods of other nations (Exod 34:12–16; Deut 6:12–15). Any relationship with a foreign nation carried the potential threat of playing the harlot with the gods of that nation.

Deuteronomy 32:16 continues: "With abominations they angered him." Here again the term "abomination" is used concerning the practice of idolatry in Deut 7:25–26; 12:30–31; 13:1–19; 17:2–5; 20:18. Deuteronomy 27:15 explicitly states, "Cursed is the man who makes an idol or a molten image, an abomination to the Lord." The term "abomination" is in apposition to the terms "molten image" and "idol." This indicates its use in connection with idolatry. Furthermore, the verb used in Deut 32:16b, כָּעַס ("to provoke to anger"), is consistently used in Deuteronomy in connection with idolatry.[3] This usage meets innertextuality criteria of similar terminology and similar context. In Deut 4:25; 9:18; 31:29; and 32:21, this verb is used to express the Israelites' predisposition to provoke the Lord to anger by pursuing other gods. These terms emphasize the context of idolatry in which Deut 32:17 is found.

---

2. Brown et al., *BDB*, 266.

3. Joo, *Provocation and Punishment*.

Deuteronomy 32:17 and Its Relationship to Exodus 32

Deuteronomy 32:17 begins with the verb זָבַח ("to sacrifice"). This verb is also found with reference to the golden calf. In Exod 32:8, God tells Moses, "They made for themselves a molten calf and bowed down to it and sacrificed to it." The use of this verb denotes a slaughter for the purpose of sacrifice.[4] It is generally used with reference to a sacrifice to the Lord but is also used of a sacrifice to false deities.[5] Its use in Deut 32:17 within a context of idolatry meets the innertextuality criteria of similar syntax and similar context, and establishes this passage as a likely innertext to the golden-calf narratives.

Directly following the verb "sacrifice," a rare Hebrew noun and an inseparable preposition occur. The combination of the noun and preposition results in the prepositional phrase לַשֵּׁדִים ("to demons").[6] The noun is only found in this passage and in Ps 106:37, where it also references the idolatrous practices of Israel.[7] Although the noun is rare, its usages in the Hebrew Bible leave little doubt to its meaning. The term suggests an image, an angelic realm within Yahwism, or a "no-god" of the surrounding nations.[8] Furthermore, early versions, including the Septuagint,[9] Vulgate, Targum Pseudo-Jonathan,[10] and Targum Neofiti 1,[11] translate the term "demon."[12]

The next clause in Deut 32:17 makes explicit the fact that these demons were false gods. It reads, "not a god, gods they did not know." It is not immediately clear whether this is a reference to the golden calf. Targum Neofiti 1 and Pseudo-Jonathan supplement the text with a term "idol." These glosses demonstrate an interpretation of the demons to be nothing other than mere images the people had produced. This interpretation would be consistent with the narrative of the golden calf.

4. Snaith, "Verbs *Zabaḥ* and *Saḥat*," 242.

5. Brown, et al., *BDB*, 256–57.

6. Ibid., 993–94.

7. Even-Shoshan, *New Concordance of the Bible*, 1114.

8. See the excursus.

9. Rahlfs, *Septuaginta*, 347.

10. Clarke, *Targum Pseudo-Jonathan: Deuteronomy*, 92. For the Aramaic, see Ginsburger, *Pseudo-Jonathan*, 359.

11. McNamara, *Targum Neofiti 1: Deuteronomy*, 154.

12. Jastrow, *Dictionary*, 1523, gives the translational equivalent of the Aramaic שֵׁידִין as "demons" and notes its sense from biblical Hebrew.

Another idol besides the golden calf is possible, however. Evidence shows that, in part, these Targumim understand this reference to the goat idols in Lev 17:7.[13] Is it possible to have both passages in mind? A closer look suggests that Deut 32:16–21 relates to Exod 32 and Levit 17.

THE RELATIONSHIP OF DEUTERONOMY 32:17 TO EXODUS 32:25

The prepositional phrase לַשֵּׁדִים ("to demons") appears intentionally related to an enigmatic phrase in Exod 32:25. In Exod 32:25, Moses sees that the people "lacked restraint because Aaron had let them loose."[14] The ensuing phrase, "for derision from the ones rising against them," is problematic for commentators. Childs indicates that even though neither of the above phrases is clear, the meaning of the verse relates to Aaron's culpability in the matter of the golden calf.[15] In the commentary by Keil and Delitzsch, the phrase is translated, "for a reproach among their foes."[16] Rashi explains it in a similar manner: "This thing would be a disgrace for them in the mouths of all those who rise against them."[17] The phrase is made difficult by the terseness of the preposition בְּ ("in") united with a plural participle of the verb קוּם ("to rise") This participle is in the construct with the third-person plural pronoun.

The sense of the phrase appears initially ambiguous. Upon closer examination, it appears that this phrase involves an *atbash* with the prepositional phrase לַשֵּׁדִים ("to demons") in Deut 32:17. An *atbash* is an abecedarian technique in substituting "for each letter in a word the letter which stands in an equivalent order in the other half of the alphabet."[18] An *aleph* is interchanged with the *taw*, a *bet* is interchanged with a *shin*, a *gimel* with a *resh*, and so on. A few *atbash* are fairly widely known. For example, Jer 25:26 and Jer 51:41 both contain the term שֵׁשַׁךְ ("Sheshach"). When the letters are interchanged by way of *atbash*, בָּבֶל ("Babel") is the result.

13. See below pp. 101–5.

14. Childs, *Book of Exodus*, 570, notes that the exact meaning of this phrase is unclear.

15. Ibid.

16. Keil and Delitzsch, *Biblical Commentary on the Old Testament*, 226–27.

17. *Mikra'ot Gedolot, Book of Exodus*, 539b.

18. Farrar, *History of Interpretation*, 102–3.

Jerome is credited with introducing this reading into Christendom.[19] In his commentary to Jeremiah, Jerome explains the Hebrew alphabet and how the city, Babylon, is arrived at by way of Sheshach.[20] In the book concerning Aphek-Antipatris, Aaron Demsky writes, "Jerome, in his commentary on the Book of Jeremiah, accepts the Jewish Hebrew *'a-t/b-s* system, which in principle, he states, is similar to the elementary practice in learning the Greek alphabet, i.e., *alpha-omega, beta-psi*."[21] Demsky, whose essay analyzes an inscription on a sherd found at Izbet Sartah, discusses the ancient abecedarian practice. He dates the inscription to the twelfth century BCE and tentatively proposes the inscription to be a student's alphabetic writing exercise. He writes, "The second and third patterns [*atbash* and *albam*] assume exercises based on the division of the twenty-two letter alphabet into two equal halves, *'alef-kaf* and *lamed-taw*. Exercises of this sort in learning the alphabet were probably as old as the order and letter names themselves and were employed in the dissemination and learning of the alphabet throughout the ancient world."[22] It appears likely that this abecedarian technique now known as *atbash* was available to the author of Deut 32:17. Moreover, being a common practice in learning the alphabet, the author would have expected his audience to recognize his play on words.

In this case, the letter B in the form בְקָמֵיהֶם ("the ones rising against them") corresponds to the שׁ in the plural term שֵׁדִים ("demons"). The letter ק corresponds to the ר, the letter מ corresponds to the י, and the letter י corresponds to the final ם in שֵׁדִים.

Using the *atbash*, the author of Deuteronomy wished to connect the worship of the golden calf with the notion of sacrificing to שֵׁדִים ("demons"). These "demons" were "no god(s)" (Deut 32:16, 21) and "vanities": הֶבֶל (Deut 32:21). The idolatry of the golden calf typifies the idolatrous ways of the people of Israel. This *atbash* provides another connection between the passages. Deuteronomy 32 continues expressing God's rejection of his people. His people have provoked him to anger and jealousy with their idolatry (Deut 32:19, 21). Because of this, he will provoke them to jealousy with another nation.

19. Ibid.
20. Jerome, *Opera*, 245.
21. Kochavi et al., *Aphek-Antipatris*, 53.
22. Ibid., 52–53.

Moreover, this connection heightens the culpability of Aaron in losing control of the people.[23] Sailhamer has shown that the compositional strategy of the Pentateuch involves several law codes.[24] These law codes are linked within the narrative framework of the Pentateuch. The incident of the golden calf demonstrates the weakness of the priesthood in restraining sin. Sailhamer writes, "By means of the arrangement of the narrative, the Sinai covenant *before the incident of the golden calf* is characterized by the laws of the Decalogue, the Covenant Code, and the instructions for building the tabernacle. However, the Sinai covenant *after the golden calf* is characterized by the fundamentally different and more extensive Code of the Priests . . . It thus appears that the incident of the golden calf has signaled a change in the nature of Israel's covenant relationship."[25] The extreme manner of Israel's sin with the golden calf necessitated restrictive laws in order to prohibit the action again.

The Relationship of Deut 32:17–21 to Deut 9:12–21

Deuteronomy 32:17 and the surrounding verses also have a linguistic connection to Deut 9:12–21. Besides the context of idolatry, the connection clearly exists in Moses' statement about the result of the golden calf. In Deut 9:18 the text gives Moses' statement, which is absent in Exodus 32.[26] Moses relates the account of his intercession and gives a summary of the sin of the people. Moses' intercession was on account of the sin "when you sinned to do evil in the eyes of the Lord to provoke him to anger." The verb כעס ("to provoke to anger") or its nominal form כעס ("provocation") is used in Deut 31:29; 32:16, 19, 21(twice), and 27. Deuteronomy 31:29 contains a recurring phrase demonstrated to have significant compositional importance.[27] In association with this phrase concerning the last days, Moses states why evil will befall them. It is because they will do evil in the eyes of the Lord, provoking him to anger with the work of their hands.[28]

---

23. Childs, *Book of Exodus*, 570.

24. Sailhamer, *Pentateuch as Narrative*, 46–47.

25. Ibid.

26. The reference to this period of intercession possibly comes from Exod 34:9. See Driver, *Deuteronomy*, 115.

27. Sailhamer, *Pentateuch as Narrative*, 35–37, 233.

28. For the phrase, "work of your hands," see Deut 4:28 and 27:15.

The subsequent four uses of this term "to provoke to anger" within Deuteronomy 32 demonstrate the prominence of the notion within the chapter. The provocation of the sons of Israel in their acts of idolatry, specifically in the idolatry of the golden calf to which Deuteronomy 9 refers, provoked the Lord to make the Israelites jealous by placing his affection on a senseless people (Deut 32:21).

LEVITICUS 17:1-7

The Relationship of Exodus 32:7-20 to Leviticus 17:7

Another passage with linguistic connections to Exodus 32 is Lev 17:1–16. In Lev 17:1–9, the Lord speaks to Moses concerning the slaughter of animals. He tells Moses to instruct Aaron, his sons, and the sons of Israel about the proper location of the sacrifice of an ox, lamb, or goat. They are to bring it to the opening of the tent of meeting in order to present it as an offering to the Lord. Anyone not doing this will be guilty of bloodshed and will be cut off from the people. The reason for this command arises from the sacrifices that were offered up in the open field. These sacrifices were not being presented at the tent of meeting to a priest. Instead they were being offered up without regulation, and consequently the people were wandering from a single devotion to God. They were sacrificing to שְׂעִירִם ("goat idols").

The terminology in this short narrative reveals some important verbal connections to Exod 32:7–20. Leviticus 17:7 makes it clear that no longer are the people to "sacrifice sacrifices to the goat idols." The verb זָבַח "sacrifice" and its nominal form, זֶבַח ("sacrifices") signal an important connection to the narrative of the golden calf. In Exod 32:8, God tells Moses that the people have made a golden calf, worshipped it, and "sacrificed" to it (זָבַח). Furthermore, this verb occurs in Deut 32:17, which also shows signs of innertextuality. This term usually denotes a slaughter for the purpose of sacrifice. In Exod 32:8 and Lev 17:7, the Israelites sacrifice to idols and commit spiritual fornication.[29]

This verb is also taken up in God's instructions to Moses in Exod 34:15. Here God warns Moses not to covenant with another nation so that the Israelites would not "play the harlot" (זנה) with their gods and

---

29. On the issue of what type of slaughter this verb denotes see Schwartz, "'Profane' Slaughter and the Integrity of the Priestly Code"; Snaith, "Verbs *Zabah* and *Sahat*," 242.

"sacrifice" (זבח) to them. In Lev 17:7, this very situation occurs. The people are sacrificing to goat idols and "playing the harlot" (זנה) with them.

The term שְׂעִירִם ("goat demon") suggests another connection. Its relationship to idolatry becomes obvious because of the next phrase in Lev 17:7. There one reads that the sons of Israel are "playing the harlot with them." *BDB* gives two translational equivalents of this term שְׂעִירִם "satyr" and "demon."[30] Its use in Isaiah (Isa 13:21, 34:14) intimates goat figures haunting the desert night.[31] The probable connection of שְׂעִירִם ("goat idol") with the term found in 2 Kgs 23:8, שְׁעָרִים ("gate"), further supports an understanding of some notion of idolatry.[32]

Early interpretation of Lev 17:7 provides instances of others who understand a connection between Lev 17:7 and the narrative of the golden calf. In 2 Chr 11:15, the term שְׂעִירִם ("goat idols") is explicitly connected with the Jeroboam's worship of עֲגָלִים ("calves").[33] The verse reads, "And he set up for himself priests for the high places and for the goat idols and for the calves which he made." This text is a near quotation of 1 Kgs 12:32.[34] In 1 Kgs 12:32, however, there is no mention of the term שְׂעִירִם ("goat idols"). It reads, "Thus he did in Bethel to sacrifice to the calves which he made and he set in Bethel priests of the high places which he made." It appears as though the author of Chronicles has intentionally inserted the term שְׂעִירִם ("goat idols"). The author of Chronicles is attempting to connect the worship of calves with the worship of goat idols.

The author of Chronicles attempts to demonstrate that the Israelites committed idolatry in the same way throughout their history as they had after the exodus. Not unlike Aaron, Jeroboam facilitated the worship of golden calves in Israel. Moreover, the author of Chronicles indicates that the worship of goat idols was also present at that time. This act of idolatry is patterned after the incident of sacrifices occurring in the fields in Leviticus 17. Israel failed to keep the very laws prohibiting idolatry, which

---

30. Brown, et al., *BDB*, 972.

31. Noth, *Leviticus*, 131.

32. Hartley, *Leviticus*, 272. See also Brown et al., *BDB*, 972; and Snaith, "Meaning of שְׂעִירִם," 116.

33. For another analysis of the relationship between the calf in Exodus and Jeroboam's calves, see Schmitt, "Die Erzählung vom Goldenen Kalb," 237–49.

34. Bendavid, *Parallels in the Bible*, 95.

are found in the Decalogue and the Covenant Code, and for which the Priestly Code and the Holiness Code were designed.[35]

The author of Chronicles is not the only early interpreter who perceived a connection between שְׂעִירִם ("goat idols") and the idolatry represented by the עֲגָלִים ("calves"). As stated above, the Targumim evince a similar connection between the idolatry to the golden calf, the שְׂעִירִם ("goat idols") and שֵׁדִים ("demons"). Targumim Onqelos, Neofiti 1, and Pseudo-Jonathan each translate the Hebrew term שְׂעִירִם ("goat idols") of Lev 17:7 with the term שֵׁדִים ("demons").[36] In doing so, each Targum likely understands the שְׂעִירִם ("goat idols") of Lev 17:7 to be equivalent to the שֵׁדִים ("demons") of Deut 32:17.

Furthermore, Leviticus Rabbah expresses that the two terms "goat idols" and "demons" are connected. In the explanation of Leviticus 17, the laws concerning the sacrifices are likened to a king who hedges up his son so that he can only eat certain objects. The explanation continues, "Similarly, because [the] Israel[ites] were passionate followers after idolatry in Egypt and used to bring their sacrifices to the satyrs . . . and these satyrs are nought but demons, as is borne out by the text which says, *They sacrificed unto demons, no-gods* (Deut. XXXII, 17), these demons being nought but satyrs, as it says, *And satyrs shall dance there* (Isa. XIII, 21)."[37] This passage obviously understands the two terms to be related. This explanation is likely understood from the fact that the context is idolatry in both passages.

Targum Pseudo-Jonathan and a marginal gloss in Targum Neofiti 1 supplement the text of Lev 17:7 with an explanatory gloss: טָעֲוָון ("idol"). Earlier in Exod 32:27, Targum Pseudo-Jonathan used this same term, טָעֲוָון ("idol"), in order to refer to the golden calf as the "idols of the nations."[38] The Targumim associate the narrative of the golden calf with the narrative of the goat idols. The author of Chronicles and early rabbinic authors give indication that others have understood this connection between passages. This suggests that a relationship between these passages has been understood traditionally and is not without warrant. What other evidence is there, however, that the passages are related within the Pentateuch?

---

35. Sailhamer, *Pentateuch as Narrative*, 46–51.

36. Jastrow, *Dictionary*, 1523.

37. Freedman and Simon, *Midrash Rabbah*, 286–87.

38. Hayward and Maher, *Targum Pseudo-Jonathan*, 52.

Another linguistic connection involves the terms מִזְבֵּחַ ("altar"), עֹלָה ("burnt offering"), and שְׁלָמִים ("peace offerings"). In the melee that followed the construction of the calf in Exodus 32, Aaron constructs an altar. The next day the people offer up burnt offerings and peace offerings. In Leviticus 17, laws are instituted so that the people will bring their offerings to the priest of the Lord and offer up a peace offering (Lev 17:5). The priest will sprinkle the blood from the animal upon the altar. Moreover, Lev 17:8 gives the consequence of disobedience. Anyone who offers up a burnt offering and does not bring it to the opening of the tent of meeting is cut off from the camp (Lev 17:8–9). These terms demonstrate a context for with religious cultic practices. In both cases (Exodus 32 and Leviticus 17) homage to false gods is central to the passage. These connections meet the criteria of similar terminology and similar context.

Another criterion for innertexuality is demonstrated with the law codes following each account of idolatry. This criterion involves similar narrative structuring features. In *The Pentateuch as Narrative*, Sailhamer discusses how Aaron was culpable in the idolatry witnessed to the golden calf. As a result the Code of the Priests from Exodus 35 to Leviticus 16 seeks to restrict the priesthood.[39]

The narrative in Leviticus 17 breaks into the Code of Priests. Although dealing with the issues of slaughter and blood, the narrative should be understood as prohibiting idolatry.[40] Furthermore, its intended addressee is not the priesthood but the common people.[41] The Lord instructs Moses to address not only Aaron and his sons but all of the sons of Israel. The sons of Israel were slaughtering animals in the open field and as a result, were falling prey to idolatry. There were no regulations restraining the people. The result is the regulation found in Leviticus 17–26, also known as the Holiness Code.[42] The juxtaposition of this block of laws with the previous narrative concerning goat idols betrays the compositional strategy within the Pentateuch. These laws were intended to restrain the sons of Israel.[43]

The type of animal required for the offering demonstrates another connection between the golden calf and the goat idols. Sailhamer has

---

39. Sailhamer, *Pentateuch as Narrative*, 47–50.

40. Rooker, *Leviticus*, 232.

41. Ibid., 230.

42. Klostermann, "Beiträge zur Entstehungsgeschichte des Pentateuchs"; Hartley, *Leviticus*, 247–48.

43. Sailhamer, *Pentateuch as Narrative*, 49–50.

pointed out the measured use of the different animals needed for the offering for a priest in contrast to any one of the sons of Israel.[44] He writes, "There appear to be intentional compositional links between the golden calf erected by the priests (עֵגֶל, Exod 32:4) and the young bull (עֵגֶל, Lev 9:1ff) required as a sin offering for the priests, and the goat idols worshiped by the people (שְׂעִיר, Lev 17:7) and the goats (שָׂעִיר, Lev 4:23) required as a sin offering for the people."[45] Sailhamer shows the calculated use of terminology in order to associate narratives with one another. This type of link between narratives and law codes demonstrates compositional strategies within those texts. These connections betray an important thematic development within the composition of the Pentateuch.

Leviticus 17:7 and Its Relationship to Deuteronomy 32:17

A possible linguistic connection between Lev 17:7 and Deut 32:17 involves a wordplay between the term שְׂעִירִם ("goat idols") and a verb used in Deut 32:17e. The last clause of Deut 32:17 can be translated, "your fathers were not acquainted with them." The term שְׂעָרוּם ("to be acquainted with") is consonantly related to the שְׂעִירִם ("goat idols") of Lev 17:7. This term is rare within biblical Hebrew and could provide a link between Lev 17:7, in which the Israelites are sacrificing to שְׂעִירִם ("goat idols"), and Deut 32:17, in which the golden calf represents שֵׁדִים ("demons").[46] The close proximity of the term שֵׁדִים ("demons") to this rare verb consonantally related to the term שְׂעִירִם ("goat idols") gives the unmistakable impression that the two passages are intentionally related.[47]

This connection between Lev 17:7 and the poetry of Deut 32:17 provides an interesting link. Deuteronomy 32:17 clearly refers to Exod 32:25 and the narrative of the golden calf. The fact that Deut 32:17 is additionally linked with Lev 17:7 demonstrates a motif within the innertextuality. An association of these four passages—Exodus 32, Leviticus 17, Deuteronomy 9, and Deuteronomy 32:15–21—exposes a focus upon the idolatrous inclination of the people of Israel.

44. Ibid., 50.

45. Ibid.

46. Brown, et al., *BDB*, 972, gives the gloss as "bristle, with horror" and lists four other examples.

47. Schwartz, "'Profane' Slaughter and the Integrity of the Priestly Code," 23, explains, "*Tg. Onq.* שְׂעִירִין connects them with the שֵׁדִים in Deut 32:17, where it is tempting to take the words לֹא שְׂעָרוּם אֲבוֹתֵיכֶם as an intentional word-play."

NUMBERS 25:1-3

The Relationship of Exodus 32:7-20 to Numbers 25:1-3

Numbers 25:1-3 reveals innertextual ties with Exod 32:7-20. Numbers 25 tells that while dwelling at Shittim, the people begin to play the harlot with the daughters of Moab. Numbers 25:2 recounts, וַתִּקְרֶאןָ לָעָם לְזִבְחֵי אֱלֹהֵיהֶן וַיֹּאכַל הָעָם וַיִּשְׁתַּחֲוּוּ לֵאלֹהֵיהֶן ("And they called to the people to the sacrifices of their gods, and the people ate, and they bowed down to their gods"). Several terms in this clause are similar to terms in Exod 32:8. First, the noun זֶבַח ("sacrifices") relates to the verbal form "sacrifice," which appears in Exod 32:8. This term has recurred in Exod 32:8; Deut 32:17; Lev 17:7; and now Num 25:2. Other occurrences can be found in related passages, such as Exod 34:15 and Deut 32:38.

The term שָׁחָה ("to bow down") can also be found in both Exodus 32 and Numbers 25. Moreover, Num 25:2 indicates that during the sacrifices, "the people ate, and they bowed down to their gods." These similar actions occur in Exod 32:6: In the midst of offering different sacrifices to the golden calf, "the people sat down to eat." Another term that recurs in both passages is אֱלֹהִים ("gods"). These connections meet the innertextuality criteria of similar terminology and similar context and establish an innertextual relationship between the two passages.

The Relationship of Numbers 25:1-3 to Leviticus 17:1-9 and Deuteronomy 31:16-30

Numbers 25:1 contains a term that establishes criteria 1 and 3. The term זָנָה ("to play the harlot") is used in Lev 17:1-9; Deut 31:16-30; and Exod 34:15-16. In each of these passages idolatry is in view. After the incident of the golden calf, God warns the people that there would be a temptation to play the harlot with the gods of conquered nations. In Lev 17:7, the people were playing the harlot after the goat idols. In Deut 31:16, the Lord indicated to Moses that after his death the people would rise up and play the harlot with other gods. This verb occurs twenty times in the Pentateuch; ten occurrences involve playing the harlot after other gods; six of those ten occurrences are associated in these innertextual passages. This use of this verb in Num 25:1; Lev 17:7; and Deut 31:16 meets the innertextuality criteria of similar terminology and similar context and establishes an innertextual connection.

DEUTERONOMY 4:12–25

Deuteronomy 9:12–21 and Its Relationship to Deuteronomy 4:12–25

Other passages within Deuteronomy also reverberate with echoes to the narrative of the golden calf. In Deuteronomy 4 Moses calls the people to obedience and devotion to the Lord. He reminds the people what happened at Mount Sinai. The people saw no form or image; instead they only heard words. God did not appear to them in a form but only in words "lest you forget and you make for yourselves an idol, the form of any image, a pattern of male or female" (Deut 4:16). Moses continues his prohibition of the construction of images. This list in Deut 4:17–19 alludes to the creation account of Genesis 1, with terms such as "animals," "birds," "creeping things," "fish," "sun," "moon," and "stars." Moses continues, reminding the people of God's deliverance from Egypt and his gift of "this good land." (Deut 4:22) The intensity grows as Moses warns the people not to "forget the covenant . . . and make for yourself an idol" (Deut 4:23).

Robert O'Connell has demonstrated the structural correspondence between Deuteronomy 4 and Deuteronomy 9.[48] O'Connell sees a rhetorical outline in which Deuteronomy 4 and 9 mirror one another.[49] Furthermore, Moshe Zipor has shown lexical correspondences between Deuteronomy 4 and 9.[50] Zipor points out that the verb שָׁחַת ("to act destructively"), the adverb מַהֵר ("quickly"), the verb in Deut 9:14 and 4:31—רָפָה—translated as "leave alone" as well as analogous subject matter such as the giving of the tablets and reference to the patriarchs all serve to tie these two chapters together.[51] Zipor concludes, "Thus, Ch. 4 contains echoes of misdeeds such as the sin of the Calf."[52] These correspondences between Deut 4:12–25; 9:12–21; and Exod 32:7–20 meet the intertextuality criteria of similar terminology, similar syntax, similar narrative features, similar context, and similar sequence of events and establish the innertextual relationship of these passages.

Moreover, on account of the golden calf, one should hear in Moses' repeated words of caution in Deut 4:23–24 a concern to avoid another

---

48. O'Connell, "Deuteronomy viii 1–20," 451–52.

49. Ibid. Particularly noteworthy is the clause, "Hear, O Israel" in 4:1 and 9:1, et al.

50. Zipor, "Deuteronomic Account of the Golden Calf," 30–31.

51. Except for the occurrence of the verb translated "leave alone" (רָפָה), all these correspondences can be seen in Exodus 32 as well.

52. Zipor, "Deuteronomic Account of the Golden Calf," 31.

lapse into idolatry. In the ensuing verses, an obvious lexical connection occurs to the narrative of the golden calf. In Deut 4:25 the phrase וַעֲשִׂיתֶם הָרַע בְּעֵינֵי יְהוָה־אֱלֹהֶיךָ לְהַכְעִיסוֹ ("and you do evil in the eyes of the Lord your God as to provoke him to anger") relates to a corresponding phrase in the narrative of the golden calf in Deut 9:18 לַעֲשׂוֹת הָרַע בְּעֵינֵי יְהוָה לְהַכְעִיסוֹ ("to do evil in the eyes of the Lord as to provoke him to anger"). [53] What is the purpose of such clausal correspondences? Such clauses reveal a pattern within the book of Deuteronomy.

These correspondences serve to tie the chapters together. G. J. Venema, in a chapter titled "The Hidden Words: Deuteronomium 9:7—10:11; 31:9–13, 24–26," writes of the connection between Deut 4 and 9,

> The "logic" behind this consequence [broken covenant] becomes instantly evident when we consider the background of this passage, given in Deut. 4:12–20, where we hear about the making of the covenant on Mount Horeb. The central fact there is that the people "out of the fire" (cf. Deut 4:12) only heard "the sound of words," but perceived no shape. Should the people nevertheless decide to make a sculptured image, "an image in any likeness whatever," they will "bring ruin upon themselves," Moses says (Deut 4:16). This is exactly what is happening here, in Deut. 9:7–17: by making a molten image the people "have brought ruin upon themselves." (Deut 9:12)[54]

Deuteronomy 4 sets the stage for the theme of rebellion and a broken covenant as it reiterates the injunctions against idolatry. It sets up the rebellion and stubbornness of Israel in the act of the golden calf. Moreover, it sets up the paradigm of Israel's tendency in the final chapters of Deuteronomy to provoke the Lord to anger.[55]

DEUTERONOMY 31:16–30

Deuteronomy 9:12–21 and Its Relationship to Deuteronomy 31:16–30

Deuteronomy 31 speaks of Moses' impending death and the transfer of leadership over to Joshua. Moses' final words are not encouraging, for he knows the people. Since he has been with them, they have been rebel-

---

53. A few Hebrew manuscripts as well as the LXX and variant readings from Kennicott preserve "your God." See Kittel et al., *Biblica Hebraica*, 302.

54. Venema, *Reading Scripture in the Old Testament*, 15–16.

55. See Deut 31:29; 32:16, 19, 21, 27.

lious and stiff necked. Why would anything change upon his death (Deut 31:28)? Indeed the Lord told Moses that this people would arise and play the harlot with other gods (Deut 31:16). The verb זָנָה ("to play the harlot") is found in other key idolatry texts within the Pentateuch, such as Exod 34:15-16 and Lev 17:7. Moreover, not unlike Deuteronomy 4 and 9, so here the covenant is at risk. Israel will play the harlot with other gods in the land where they are going. They will forsake God and break the covenant that God cut with them.

Moshe Zipor has pointed out other connections to the golden calf. The uses of the terms "rebellious" and "stiff-necked" have marked use in connection with the golden calf.[56] The verb שָׁחַת ("to act destructively") has been demonstrated above to be associated with the golden calf in Exod 32:7 and in Deut 4:16, 4:25, and 9:26; now it appears in Deut 31:29.

Zipor points out other similarities with Deut 31:28-29. He writes,

> In addition, other expressions of 31, 28-29 seem to refer to the exhortations, either in 9-10, 11, or in Ch. 4:
>
>> and I shall call heaven and earth to witness against them (cfr. 4,26)
>> for I know that after my death you will surely act destructively (cfr. 4,16.25; 9,12)
>> and turn aside from the way which I have commanded you (cfr. 9,12; Ex 32,8)
>> and in the days to come evil will befall you (cfr. 4,30)
>> because you will do what is evil in the sight of the Lord
>> provoking him to anger through the work of your hands (cfr. 4,25; 9,18)[57]

Zipor's analysis conclusively ties Deuteronomy 31 to the incident of idolatry to the golden calf. A few more details can be added.

Deut 4:25 and 9:18 along with Deut 31:29 have almost the exact clause תַּעֲשׂוּ אֶת־הָרַע בְּעֵינֵי יְהוָה לְהַכְעִיסוֹ ("you did evil in the eyes of the Lord so as to provoke him to anger"). The use of this clause and, in particular, of the term כָּעַס ("to provoke to anger") has been shown above to be an important term in the book of Deuteronomy and will reveal troublesome consequences in the Song of Moses in Deuteronomy 32.

Another significant feature of Deut 31:29 involves a connection to Deut 4:30. Both these verses include the important phrase בְּאַחֲרִית הַיָּמִים

56. Zipor, "Deuteronomic Account of the Golden Calf," 31-32.
57. Ibid., 32.

("in the last days"). Sailhamer has demonstrated the significance of this phrase in conjunction with the poetic seams in other key passages within the Pentateuch, such as Gen 49:1 and Num 24:14. Its use here in Deut 31:29 and in Deut 4:30 can hardly be accidental, and suggests a subtle reminder of events that will surround these idolatrous days.[58]

The final phrase in Deut 31:29 ("the work of your hands") likewise evokes a theme of idolatry. This phrase was also used in Deut 4:28, in which Moses speaks of the "last days" (Deut 4:30) when the Israelites would be scattered among the nations and serve gods, the work of the hands of man The theme of idolatry reverberates through the book of Deuteronomy as if there were some hope that the warnings would be heeded. And yet the Song of Moses makes clear that the Lord would make Israel jealous of another nation, just as Israel has made God jealous of other, false gods (Deut 32:16–21). These connections between Deut 31:16–30; Exod 32:7–20; Lev 17:1–7; Deut 4:12–25; 9:12–21; and 32:16–21 establish these passages as innertextuality.

This section has applied the innertextuality criteria of association to Exod 32:7–20; Lev 17:1–7; Deut 4:12–25; Deut 9:12–21; Deut 31:16–30; and Deut 32:16–21, and has established these passages as innertextually related. The connections have provided a focus on Israel's rebellion, their idolatry, the breaking of the covenant, and the Lord's provoking them through a senseless nation. The conclusion will state the results and implications of this analysis.

58. Sailhamer, *Introduction to Old Testament Theology*, 210–11.

Excursus: Idolatry in the Pentateuch

THE SIN OF IDOLATRY emerges as a prominent theme in the Old Testament. This analysis has demonstrated the importance of the theme of idolatry within the composition of the Pentateuch. The precise nature of idolatry, however, remains in question. The answer to this question is necessary for biblical theology and could provide a better understanding to the development of the religion of Israel. A study of religion in the Ancient Near East suggests both similarities and dissimilarities with the religion of Israel. The texts of the Bible play an influential role in discerning the religion of Israel and the nature of idolatry.

The Pentateuch holds several injunctions against idolatry. The discussion of these injunctions below will elucidate the polemic against idolatry. Several fundamental questions remain. Was the injunction against idolatry opposed to the use of images for *Yahweh*? Or was the injunction opposed to the use of images for other gods? What did the authors of Scripture intend when they prohibited the worship of other gods? Did they have in mind a personal being when they banned idol production and the worship of gods? Or was it only fetishism?[1] In *The Religion of Ancient Israel*, Patrick Miller frames the discussion concerning the production of images.

> Here we come upon one of the distinctive features of the worship of *Yahweh* in ancient Israel—its aniconic character. The absence of images of the deity and the concomitant prohibition against representation of deity in any form of image is anomalous in the

---

1. Kaufmann, *Religion of Israel*, 13, 14. Fetishism is "the belief that divine and magical powers inhere in certain natural or man-made objects and that man can activate these powers through fixed rituals. These objects, upon which magical rituals are performed, are 'the gods of the nations.' The Bible does not conceive the powers as personal beings who dwell in the idols; the idol is not a habitation of the god, it is the god himself. Hence the oft-repeated biblical stigmatization of the pagan gods as 'wood and stone,' 'silver and gold.' Hence also its sole polemical argument that idolatry is the senseless deification of wood and stone images" (14).

ancient Near East. The creation and use of images in the cultus was ubiquitous in the religions of that time and place. For the most part in Israel, they were not present and were officially inveighed against. Three questions about this unusual phenomenon are the subject of considerable debate: (1) Was the prohibition of images directed primarily toward images of *Yahweh* or images of other gods? (2) When did the prohibition against images actually begin? Was there a time when images were permissible in the worship of *Yahweh*? (3) What was the function or meaning of this aniconic feature? Why were images not used and not permitted? An attempt to answer these questions will uncover at least some of the dimension of this rather unique feature of *Yahwism*.[2]

Miller discusses this aniconic feature of Israel's religion and its relationship to the religions of the surrounding nations. An understanding of this feature, along with a comprehension of how the biblical texts portray the actuality of other personal gods, will reveal the precise nature of idolatry from a biblical point of view.

In the ensuing discussion, the following issues will guide the discussion: (1) Did the injunction against idol making only ban images of other gods or did it ban all images including images representing *Yahweh*? (2) Do the biblical texts reveal any acknowledgement of the existence of other actual deities? The next section will examine the biblical injunctions against idolatry and those texts associated with idolatry in order to arrive at an understanding of the precise nature of idolatry within the Pentateuch.

INJUNCTIONS AGAINST IDOLATRY

The injunctions against idolatry reveal a disposition against any production of images.[3] Furthermore, they provide evidence that the biblical writers did not consider the existence of other deities as valid. The following passages within the Pentateuch contain commands against the production of images: Exod 20:3–6, 23; 34:17; Lev 19:4; 26:1; Deut 4:16, 23; 5:6–10; and 27:15. In each of these passages, there is a command not to make an image. For example, Exod 20:4 says, "You shall not make for

2. Miller, *Religion of Ancient Israel*, 15.

3. The following Hebrew terms are able to connote an idolatrous image or object: מַסֵּכָה בָּמָה בַּעַל אֱלֹהִים אֵלִים הֶבֶל אֱלִילִים שִׁקּוּץ גִּלּוּלִים חָמָן תְּרָפִים צֶלֶם פֶּסֶל פָּסִיל עֶצֶב. Taken in part from Meadors, *Idolatry and the Hardening of the Heart*, 12–13.

yourself an idol or any image which is in the heavens above or which is in the earth below or which is in the waters under the earth." In certain passages, there is an even more specific injunction against the production of any image (Deut 4:16, 23, 25; 5:8). For example, Deut 4:23 says, "And you shall not make for yourself an idol in the form of anything which the Lord your God has commanded you." In all of these commands, the prohibition against the production of an image is clear.

Deuteronomy 4:10–19 explains further that the Lord did not appear to them at Mount Sinai in any form. They saw no form and instead heard only a voice. This occurred so that they should not be tempted to make any image. This passage asserts then that the production of any image, including any image representing Yahweh is disallowed.

The incident of the golden calf presents a questionable scenario. Is the condemnable idolatry of the golden calf to be understood as the production of an image which represented another deity? Or was it the production of an image which represented the one true God, *Yahweh*? In his work *The Pentateuch as Narrative*, John Sailhamer listed several reasons why the incident of the golden calf was a case of idolatry and not polytheism. He writes,

> First, that the people wanted Aaron to "make" a god(s) for them (v. 1) shows that the term *'elohim* was understood as something that could be made—an idol, not a deity as such . . . Second, the Hebrew word for "idol" (מַסֵּכָה) is actually used in this passage to describe the "god" that Aaron made . . . Third, Aaron fashioned only one golden calf. It is not likely that one calf would be called "gods" (in the plural) if actual gods were to be understood. Thus the reference to a single calf suggests that it represented one god/God and not many gods. Fourth, the "god" (*'elohim*) which Aaron made is always referred to with the singular pronoun "it." Finally, the celebration of the making of the golden calf is called "a feast for the LORD." (v.5)[4]

To these observations, one could note three additional remarks. First, in both Exodus 32 and Deuteronomy 9, the golden calf is destroyed. The calf is pulverized, thrown into water, and the object is seemingly annihilated. In connection with this, there is no reference to any deity within entire narrative. This would suggest that the image of the calf which has been

---

4. Sailhamer, *Pentateuch as Narrative*, 311.

crafted was the forbidden deed and not the creation nor the worship of an actual deity.

Second, in the portrayal of the incident in Deuteronomy 9, there is a direct connection between the production of the golden calf and the text of Deuteronomy 4. Deuteronomy 9:15 and Deut 4:11 both contain the exact phrase וְהָהָר בֹּעֵר בָּאֵשׁ ("And the mountain was burning with fire"). In Deut 4:10–16, Moses explained to the people that God spoke to them from the midst of the fire without seeing any form so that they would not act corruptly and make any image. Deuteronomy 9:15 is connected to Deut 4:10–16 by the above phrase. This association between the two passages betrays the fact that they have produced an image even though they saw none. This connection suggests that the image of the golden calf represents the one who spoke to them from the midst of the fire.

Third, Deut 9:18 says, "And I fell before the Lord as at first, forty days and forty nights, I neither ate bread nor drank water because of all your sin which you committed to do evil in the eyes of the Lord to provoke him to anger." The phrase "to provoke to anger" is used in connection with idolatry in Deut 4:25; 9:18; 31:29; 32:16, 19, and 21. It illustrates the rebellious character of the people and their consistent refusal to obey the command concerning idolatry. In each case, idolatry is immediately in view. Moreover, Deut 31:29 says, "Because I know after my death that you will surely act corruptly and turn aside from the way which I commanded you and evil with befall you in the latter days because you did evil in the eyes of the Lord to provoke him to anger with the work of your hands." This passage has terminological and clausal connections to the text of Deut 9:12–21. The phrases "to provoke to anger," "act corruptly," and "turn aside from the way which I commanded you" connect Deut 31:29 to the incident in Deuteronomy 9. Deuteronomy 31:29 obviously has idolatry in view—and not polytheism, because of the phrase "with the work of your hands." As a result of these connections, the incident of the golden calf in Deuteronomy 9 is portrayed in the Pentateuch as idolatry and not polytheism.

The passages that ban the production of images contain other elements which could suggest that idolatry involves another god. Exodus 20:3–5 says, "You shall have no other gods before me. You shall not make for yourself an idol or any image which is in the heavens above or which is in the earth below or which is in the waters under the earth. You shall not bow down to them and you shall not serve them." What does the term "gods" mean if not an actual deity? The fact that the Israelites bowed down to them and served them could imply a personal deity. The terminology, however, suggests otherwise. The term אֱלֹהִים ("gods") denotes both the true God of Israel as well as the false gods with whom Israel played the harlot. Sailhamer writes, "[T]he Hebrew expression "other gods" (אֱלֹהִים אֲחֵרִים) or "gods" (אֱלֹהִים) is often, if not always, used specifically as a term for idols and not, as we might have expected, for "other gods" per se. In Deut 28:36, for example, the expression "other gods" clearly refers not to other deities as such but to "gods of wood and stone," that is, idols."[5] The term אֱלֹהִים "gods" refers not to an actual deity but to an image.

In each of the injunctions against the production of images, the term עָשָׂה "to make" is important. This term shows that the biblical writers considered an idol as something that is made, not an actual deity that exists. Moreover, the context in each of the injunctions against idolatry, Exod 20:3–6, 23; 34:17; Lev 19:4; 26:1; Deut 4:16, 23; 5:6–10; and 27:15, contains limiting terminology. Terms such as "molten image," "gods of silver and gods of gold," "the form of anything," or "the work of hands" limit the idol to something that is made and not an actual deity. Furthermore, in none of these passages are these terms said to represent an actual, named deity.[6]

TEXTS ASSOCIATED WITH IDOLATRY

A number of other passages are associated with idolatry in a different manner. These passages associate the people of Israel with idolatry through either a condemnation for idolatry or a warning against future idolatry. The issue remains whether or not these passages reveal a polytheistic outlook. Is it possible that the gods of other nations with whom Israel played the harlot are considered gods alongside the God of Israel? The discussion below will examine these passages in light of this question. A consideration of these passages indicates a polemic against fetishism rather than polytheism.

The main passages which condemn or warn Israel for idolatry are Exod 20:3–5; 22:19; 34:12–17; Lev 17:7; Num 25:1–3; Deut 4:15–35; 5:6–10; 7:2–5, 16, 25–26; 11:16, 28; 12:2–3, 30–31; 13:1–15; 16:21–22; 17:2–3; 18:9–14; 20:17–18; 27:15; 28:36; 29:17–18, 25; 30:17; 31:16–20,

---

5. Ibid., 310–11.

6. Kaufmann, *Religion of Israel,* 9, 11, 60–63.

29; and 32:16–21. These passages typically involve sacrificing to, playing the harlot with, bowing down to, or serving other gods. In many of these cases, the gods to which the idolatry is committed are natural objects. For example, Deut 4:28 says, "And there you will serve gods, the work of man's hands, wood and stone, which cannot see nor hear nor eat nor smell." In these cases, the "god(s)" does not represent an actual deity but is the object of veneration itself.

Moreover, Deut 4:39 makes clear the biblical view of any deity other than *Yahweh*. It says, "And you should know today and take it to your heart that the Lord, he is God in the heavens above and on the earth below; there is no other." This verse reveals the biblical polemic against any other deity to which rival the Lord. These passages associated with idolatry, consequently, should be understood as fetishism rather than polytheism.

Two of the above passages, however, require a further comment. These passages seem to imply not only iconography but activity in the spirit realm. Deuteronomy 18:9–14 warns the people of Israel against practices of sorcery, divination, magic, spiritism, and soothsaying. Instead, God would raise up for Israel a prophet who would command Israel in the Lord's ways (Deut 18:15–18). These other ways of seeking the divine will were prohibited in Israel but show that unorthodox ways of attaining powers and knowledge existed alongside appropriate ways of finding God's will.[7] This activity is not polytheistic, however. Instead it reveals activity that was syncretistic or activity that was practiced within Yahwism but was eventually prohibited.[8]

The other passage which suggests spirit activity but falls short of polytheism is Deut 32:16–21. Deuteronomy 32:17 uses the term שֵׁדִים ("demons"). This term suggests more than an idolatrous image but cannot be used to support any deistic being.[9] Kaufmann conceives of this and other references to demonic activity (Lev 17:7 et al.) as a feature of Yahwism.[10] All activity in the angelic realm ultimately comes from *Yahweh*.[11]

Also, the context of Deut 32:16–21 requires that the "demons" be nothing that can rival God. They are "not a god" (Deut 32:16, 21).

7. Miller, *Religion of Ancient Israel*, 54–55.

8. Ibid., 54–56.

9. Kaufmann, *Religion of Israel*, 64–65.

10. Ibid., 8–11, 18, 63–67.

11. Volz, *Dämonische in Jahwe*, 32.

Moreover, they are הֶבֶל ("vanities"), idols in whom there is no existence. The people of Israel had wasted their devotion on images which had no real being.

CONCLUSION

There is much attention devoted to the notion of idolatry within the Pentateuch. The nature of idolatry consists of homage paid to a mere natural or man-made object. There is no god that rivals *Yahweh*. The gods of the nations are not portrayed as deities with whom the true God of Israel duals. The people had provoked the Lord through devotion to mere images and falsehoods.

4

Conclusion

THIS CHAPTER WILL STATE the results and implications of this study in the following areas of research: 1) the unity of the Pentateuch, 2) hermeneutics and innerbiblical exegesis and allusion, 3) the theology of the Pentateuch, and 4) general biblical studies. It will also suggest directions for further research in light of the results reached in this analysis.

RESULTS AND IMPLICATIONS FOR THE UNITY
OF THE PENTATEUCH

This section will indicate the results and implications for the unity of the Pentateuch in view of the innertextuality between Exod 32:7–20; Deut 9:12–21; Deut 32:16–21; Lev 17:1–7; Num 25:1–3; Deut 4:12–25; and Deut 31:16–30. It will do so by first discussing the intentional and interpretive nature of the connection between Exod 32:7–20 and Deut 9:12–21. Second, it will discuss the innertextuality between Exod 32:7–20; Deut 9:12–21; Deut 32:16–21; Lev 17:1–7; Num 25:1–3; Deut 4:12–25; and Deut 31:16–30 and the implications these innertexts have on the unity of the Pentateuch.

The Intentional Connection between Exodus 32:7–20
and Deuteronomy 9:12–21

Innertextuality is the intentional connection between texts in order to combine them into a larger whole. A connection consists of formal linguistic elements that exist in two or more passages. Chapter 1 listed nine criteria that establish an intentional connection between passages. Chapter 2 demonstrated how the connections between Exod 32:7–20 and Deut 9:12–21 meet seven of these criteria in numerous instances and consistent fashion. This analysis has demonstrated that an intentional connection exists between Exod 32:7–20 and Deut 9:12–21.

It is quite clear that in the final shape of the Pentateuch Exod 32:7–20 and Deut 9:12–21 were composed in relationship to one another. Figure 1 and the catalogue of clauses, phrases, and terminology showed the overwhelming agreement of particular clauses, phrases, and terminology between the passages. This agreement demonstrates that the relationship between these two passages is intentional and can be examined for further meaning. Furthermore, their inclusion into the texts of Exodus and Deuteronomy respectively links these texts together and provokes further study related to the association between Exodus and Deuteronomy.

This formal link between Exodus and Deuteronomy, especially within the narrative framework of Moses' explaining the *Torah* (Deut 1:5), has important implications for the unity and interpretation of the Pentateuch. Its implications for the unity of the Pentateuch are as follows: when understood in light of the intentional connection between Exod 32:7–20 and Deut 9:12–20 and the narrative framework in Deut 1:5, this relationship suggests that text of Deuteronomy is in composition with the other texts of the Pentateuch. The one responsible for the final shape of the Pentateuch brought these texts in relationship to one another and expects them to be understood as a unity.

Its implications for the interpretation of the Pentateuch are as follows: When understood in light of the intentional connection between Exod 32:7–20 and Deut 9:12–20 this relationship suggests that Deuteronomy is in composition with the other texts of the Pentateuch in order to comment on or interpret those texts in the Pentateuch which come before it. These connected texts comment upon and apply the meaning of the previous texts in a distinct manner. This aspect of the text of Deuteronomy commenting on the *narrative* in Exodus can be clearly seen in the formal connection between Exod 32:7–20 and Deut 9:12–21. Deuteronomy 1:5 states that Moses is explaining the *Torah*. This analysis makes evident that Deuteronomy 9 is explaining the text of Exod 32:7–20 and is not explaining law codes nor is it a mere recapitulation from memory.

This section has stated the implications for the unity of the Pentateuch in view of the intentional connection of Exod 32:7–20 and Deut 9:12–21. It has done so by stating the results of the comparison between the two passages and in view of the narrative framework in Deut 1:5.

Innertextuality between Exodus 32:7–20, Deuteronomy 9:12–21,
Deuteronomy 32:16–21, Leviticus 17:1–7, Numbers 25:1–3,
Deuteronomy 4:12–25, and Deuteronomy 31:16–30

Another feature of innertextuality is its distribution of connected texts throughout a larger whole. The connections between texts thus serve to bind these texts together into a unity. Chapter 3 demonstrated the intentional connection of Exod 32:7–20 and Deut 9:12–21 to Deut 32:16–21; Lev 17:1–7; Num 25:1–3; Deut 4:12–25; and Deut 31:16–30. It did so by applying criteria to these passages and establishing an intentional connection. The connections between these passages indicate a distribution throughout the Pentateuch. Thus these passages are in an innertextual relationship with one another. Furthermore, because of their distribution throughout the whole, the unity of the Pentateuch can be seen.

Interestingly, these passages involve texts that have traditionally been assigned to different sources of the Documentary Hypothesis. This innertextuality demonstrates the utilization of connected textual units spanning across classical designations of texts. The results show the inadequacy of the Documentary Hypothesis to accommodate the composition demonstrated in this analysis. In one popular understanding of the Documentary Hypothesis, the innertextual passages discussed in this analysis have been assigned to the following sources:[1] Exod 32:7–20 is from the Elohist; Lev 17:1–7 is from the Priestly document; Num 25:1–3 is from the Yahwist; Deut 4:12–25, 9:12–21, 31:16–22, 32:17 are from Deuteronomy. Regardless of their origin, however, the innertextuality between these passages demonstrates that they have been composed into a unity. This composition spans these alleged sources and makes evident the unity of the Pentateuch.

The innertextuality demonstrated between these passages demonstrates that the final shape of the Pentateuch constitutes a compositional unity. The author has intentionally included these texts in relationship to one another in order to structure his text in a meaningful and purposeful manner. This unity helps delineate the boundaries of the Pentateuch as a focus for further study. This section has discussed the implications of the innertextuality between Exod 32:7–20; Deut 9:12–21; Deut 32:16–21; Lev

---

1. Friedman, *Bible with Sources Revealed*. These designations are taken from a recent attempt to synthesize the findings of source criticism in Friedman's own translation of the Pentateuch.

17:1–7; Num 25:1–3; Deut 4:12–25; and Deut 31:16 –30 as it relates to the unity of the Pentateuch.

RESULTS AND IMPLICATIONS FOR HERMENEUTICS AND INNERBIBLICAL EXEGESIS AND ALLUSION

This section will indicate the results and implications for hermeneutics and innerbiblical exegesis and allusion in view of the innertextuality between Exod 32:7–20; Deut 9:12–21; Deut 32:16–21; Lev 17:1–7; Num 25:1–3; Deut 4:12–25; and Deut 31:16 –30 and the methodology used to establish this innertextuality. It will do so in four steps. First, it will discuss the intentional connection between Exod 32:7–20 and Deut 9:12–21 and its implication for hermeneutics and innerbiblical exegesis and allusion. Second, it will discuss the innertextuality between Exod 32:7–20; Deut 9:12–21; Deut 32:16–21; Lev 17:1–7; Num 25:1–3; Deut 4:12–25; and Deut 31:16 –30 and its implications for hermeneutics and innerbiblical exegesis and allusion. Third, it will discuss the methodology and criteria which established the intentional connection between Exod 32:7–20 and Deut 9:12–21. Fourth, it will discuss the significance this analysis has in relationship to composition and an understanding of biblical authorship.

The Intentional Connection between Exodus 32:7–20 and Deuteronomy 9:12–21

Hermeneutics can be understood as the science of interpreting texts. Most scholars acknowledge that a legitimate approach to the interpretation of texts is based on the makeup and purpose of the text under investigation. By establishing criteria of association and demonstrating that Exod 32:7–20 and Deut 9:12–21 have clearly met those criteria, this analysis has shown that these texts were composed in relationship to one another. Moreover, the intentional connection between the two passages indicates a purpose in that relationship. Thus, in order to interpret these texts according to their makeup and purpose, one should consider the relationship between the two passages.

Innerbiblical exegesis and allusion examine the way in which texts relate to one another. Innerbiblical exegesis, synchronic and diachronic studies, methodology which ascertains dependence between two texts, and the relationship of the New Testament to the Old Testament are areas in which the relationship of one text to another is currently being considered within scholarship. The intentional connection between Exod 32:7–20 and Deut 9:12–21 reveals an instance of textual relationship. The results of the analysis are a solid basis on which to consider the nature of the relationship and the purpose for which it was composed. This analysis has not only demonstrated an intentional connection but has attempted to explain the purpose for which it was constructed in view of its intentionality and the narrative framework of Deuteronomy. This analysis has established criteria to determine an intentional relationship and applied those criteria to Exod 32:7–20 and Deut 9:12–21.

Innertextuality between Exodus 32:7–20; Deuteronomy 9:12–21;
Deuteronomy 32:16–21; Leviticus 17:1–7; Numbers 25:1–3;
Deuteronomy 4:12–25; and Deuteronomy 31:16–30

The innertextuality between Exod 32:7–20; Deut 9:12–21; Deut 32:16–21; Lev 17:1–7; Num 25:1–3; Deut 4:12–25; and Deut 31:16–30 has certain implications for hermeneutics and innerbiblical exegesis and allusion. This analysis has demonstrated results that 1) show that these passages were intentionally connected to one another. In demonstrating this, the connections have provided a focus for which the passages were linked together; 2) show that the passages were combined into a larger whole. In demonstrating this, the connections show the unity of the Pentateuch. It is commonly recognized that the boundaries and unity of a text have relevance for verbal meaning. As a result, both the way in which innertextuality is demonstrated and any results of its application should be taken into consideration.

This analysis demonstrated innertextuality by applying criteria to different passages that show signs of relationship. Criteria establish that the connections between the passages are formal. These connections provide the focus for which reason the passages are innertexted. These formal connections exhibit similarities between any innertexted passages. As a result of the similarities, the immediate literary contexts of the individual innertexts also show divergences. These divergences can then be examined for interpretive significance. This work provides a model for how innertextuality provides the focus for which the passages were associated with one another and how divergences can be examined for interpretive value.

Conclusion

The results of the analysis demonstrate the unity of a text which has been generated through the connections between passages. This work has shown the composition of the Pentateuch through the interrelationship of these passages. As a result, the work examined the innertexts in order to discern the purpose for their composition in the Pentateuch. It has done so in view of the relationship between the innertexts and in particular, the significant chapter of Deuteronomy 32. This chapter is significant because it represents an approximate boundary to the Pentateuch both traditionally as well as through the demonstration of this analysis. This analysis has attempted to provide an example of interpreting particular innertexted passages within a compositional unity.

Methodology and Criteria in Establishing an Intentional Connection

The need for criteria to establish an intentional connection has received recent attention. The reason involves the development of structuralist, post-structuralist, and reader-response approaches to the interpretation of texts. Criteria may be used to establish an intentional basis for which a text is associated with another text. An examination of texts which endeavors to find a meaning must deal with intentionality. This analysis attempts to establish a method which applies criteria in a formal manner. In doing so, it attempts to discern the intentions embodied in a text by means an examination of those texts. It looks for formal patterns which exceed coincidence; thus grounding interpretation in those patterns. The criteria used in this analysis are the following: similar terminology, similar syntax, similar narrative features, similar thematic contexts, similar sequence of events, repetition of structure, contextual awareness, breaking a recognizable pattern, and shifting connotation.

The application of these criteria to other texts can be done in order to discern an intentional connection in those texts. These criteria make no claim to be exhaustive. Other texts may exhibit different patterns which point to intentionality. Other criteria can be established based on the examination of other texts. Ultimately, the criteria must establish that a connection was intentional. Some criteria establish a stronger attestation than others. These criteria, however, provide an initial point at which to begin an investigation.

Composition and Biblical Authorship

The innertextuality established in this analysis shows how an author selected, arranged, adapted, and wrote distinct individual textual units in order to compose his text. It did so by demonstrating the reuse, the organization and distribution, the adaptation of particular textual units, and the possible generation of textual units. The reuse of particular textual units was made evident in the similar or identical makeup of the connected elements. The fact that the textual units were similar or identical evinces that they were reused. It was not by coincidence that the same textual unit appears repeatedly. This reuse establishes the notion of selection. Selection of textual units on the basis of an author's purpose is an aspect of composition.

The organization and distribution of particular textual units were revealed in two cases. The first case involves the way in which each passage organized the different textual units. Each passage had material that was limited to that single passage. This material limited to a single passage makes obvious that the reused textual units are organized in a distinct manner in each passage. Otherwise the two passages would be absolutely identical. The fact that they are not evinces distinct organization in each case. This case of organization establishes the notion of arrangement and is consistent with the notion of composition.

The other case involves the way in which a similar textual unit is distributed throughout the Pentateuch. This distribution throughout a text shows how certain textual units are arranged. This case of distribution establishes the notion of arrangement and is consistent with the notion of composition.

The adaptation and writing of a particular textual unit is apprehended when textual units are transposed based on the purpose of the author. Moreover, a textual unit is generated in order to produce a desired effect. A case in point is the relationship between Exod 32:20 and Deut 9:21 respectively. In this verse, the same textual units with the exception of "your sin" are used but they are transposed; a lexeme in second position is moved to third position; a lexeme in first position is moved to fourth position; a lexeme in third position is moved to second position. The same lexemes are used in both passages. The author likely had the same textual unit with which to compose both passages. He adapted the textual unit, however, to suit his purposes and generated a further effect through the noun phrase "your sin." The adaptation and writing of textual units is an aspect of composition.

This section has indicated the results and implications for hermeneutics and innerbiblical exegesis and allusion in view of the innertextuality between Exod 32:7–20; Deut 9:12–21; Deut 32:16–21; Lev 17:1–7; Num 25:1–3; Deut 4:12–25; and Deut 31:16–30 and the methodology used to establish this innertextuality. It has done so by discussing the intentional connection between Exod 32:7–20 and Deut 9:12–21, the innertextuality between Exod 32:7–20; Deut 9:12–21; Deut 32:16–21; Lev 17:1–7; Num 25:1–3; Deut 4:12–25; and Deut 31:16–30, the methodology and criteria which established the intentional connection between Exod 32:7–20 and Deut 9:12–21, and the composition and an understanding of biblical authorship.

RESULTS AND IMPLICATIONS FOR THE THEOLOGY OF THE PENTATEUCH

This section will indicate the results and implications for the theology of the Pentateuch in view of the innertextuality between Exod 32:7–20; Deut 9:12–21; Deut 32:16–21; Lev 17:1–7; Num 25:1–3; Deut 4:12–25; and Deut 31:16–30. It will do so in three ways. First, it will discuss the intentional connection between Exod 32:7–20 and Deut 9:12–21 and the purposes for that connection. Second, it will discuss the innertextuality between the passages and its coherence with the compositional strategies within the Pentateuch. Third, it will utilize the results of this analysis in order to contribute to the contemporary expression of the theology of the Pentateuch.

Purposes for the Intentional Connection between Exodus 32:7–20 and Deuteronomy 9:12–21

Chapter 2 applied the criteria of association to these two passages in order to establish an intentional relationship between them. The relationship exposes the similarities and divergences between the two passages. The similarities provide the focus of the connections while certain divergences cohere either with the immediate context of an individual passage or within the compositional strategies of the Pentateuch.

The similarities center upon the sin of the Israelites in the production of the molten calf. The passages approximately agree in the Lord's command to Moses to go quickly because the people who had come out of Egypt had acted corruptly and turned aside from God's command not to produce an image. The passages come together again at the Lord's pronouncement of the Israelites' character: they were stiff-necked. Consequently, the Lord would destroy them and make Moses into a great nation. After an unparalleled portion in Exod 32:11–14, the passages agree again to show Moses coming from the mountain. After another unparalleled portion in Exod 32:15d–19a, the passages converge upon the scene of Moses' initial view of the calf and his smashing of the tablets. This time an unparalleled portion occurs in Deut 9:18–20 before the passages approximately join with one another a final time over the destruction of the calf.

In Deuteronomy 9, noticeably absent from these similarities is the intercession of Moses and the Lord's reprieve from destruction. In Exodus 32, Moses' intercession includes a reference to the Lord's deliverance from Egypt, the Egyptians' response to the Israelite's destruction, the covenant with Abraham, Isaac, and Israel along with the named blessings. Moreover, one finds no extended discussion in Deuteronomy 9 of the tablets of the testimony nor does one find the scene of Moses and Joshua approaching the idolatrous episode.

Because of the intentional connection demonstrated from the criteria, one is able to deduce that these textual units are not of primary significance for the arrangement in Deuteronomy. The character of the people of Israel, the production and destruction of the calf, and the smashing of the tablets remain the focus in the connections. When viewed from the perspective of all the innertexts, one can see the convergence of similar terms and themes. The terms and themes converge on image making, sacrificing and playing the harlot to other gods, the sin and stiff-necked character of the people, the breaking of the covenant, and God provoking Israel to jealousy by embracing a senseless nation.

The arrangement in Deuteronomy 9 centers upon the corruptible action of the people and in two occasions indicates their quick rebellion in turning away from the Lord's command. The passage most certainly emphasizes the production of the calf: the phrase "which they/you made a calf, a molten image," recurs three times. On four occasions, nominal and verbal forms for the term חָטָא "sin" occur between Deut 9:12–21 without occurring once in Exod 32:7–20. The sin and stiff-necked character of the people are repeatedly the center of attention in Deuteronomy 9.

Furthermore, the Lord's plan to destroy them, wipe out their name from under heaven and make Moses an even greater nation appears as an ominous sign for the future of the people. The destruction of the tablets becomes an occasion for the breach of the covenant and the idol is repeatedly pulverized as if to indicate the absolute despicable nature the entire episode.

The divergences limited to the account in Deuteronomy 9 cohere both with the immediate context of Deuteronomy and within the inner-texted passages. The immediate context of Deuteronomy portrays Moses' sharp warning to the people. They had been rebellious since the day they had left Egypt (Deut 9:7) and rebellious since the day Moses knew them (Deut 9:24). They had consistently provoked the Lord to anger with their idolatry and their rebellious tendency (Deut 9:22–23).

The Innertextual Passages and Their Coherence with Compositional Passages within the Pentateuch

This section will give the results of the analysis concerning innertextuality and show how those results cohere within the compositional strategies within the Pentateuch. Chapter 3 applied criteria of association to other passages within the Pentateuch that showed signs of innertextuality. The innertexted passages include Exod 32:7–20; Deut 9:12–21; Deut 32:16–21; Lev 17:1–7; Num 25:1–3; Deut 4:12–25; and Deut 31:16–30. Criteria 1–6 were clearly met. These innertexts develop the motif of Israel's continual apostasy and its strain upon the covenant. In each case, a view to Israel's present or future apostasy is the focus. Each instance reverberates with the incident of the golden calf. Moreover, in each case, the covenant is in question as a result of the apostasy and the destruction of the Israelites either occurs or is threatened. The motifs of apostasy, breaking the covenant, and the role of Israel in God's future plan become important notions within the composition of the Pentateuch.

Contribution to Contemporary Expressions of the Theology of the Pentateuch

This section will suggest how the results of this analysis can contribute the theology of the Pentateuch. The results of this analysis demonstrate the importance of the innertextuality associated with the idolatry of the golden calf. The importance lies not in the event itself, nor even in the narrative portrayal of that event but its exemplary quality manifested by the numerous innertexts. The innertextuality shows that within the composition of the Pentateuch, the apostasy of the people plays an influential role.

Moreover, the influence of these innertexts can be understood not only in view of God's relationship to Israel in the past, in that event at Sinai, but also to the future. The development of the compositional strategies throughout the Pentateuch and to its conclusion in Deuteronomy makes clear that the apostasy of the people influences their covenantal relationship to God. When followed to its conclusion in Deut 32:16–21, the innertextuality between these passages clearly develops the notion that God will provoke Israel to jealousy with another nation. Deuteronomy 32:21 says, "They have made me jealous with not a god, they have provoked me to anger with vanities. So I, I will make them jealous with not a people, with a senseless nation, I will provoke them." Deuteronomy 32:17–21 appears to encapsulate the innertextuality. Israel had constantly fallen prey to idolatry and embraced false gods. Because of this God would provoke them to jealousy by embracing another nation.

This section has applied the results and implications of the innertextuality between Exod 32:7–20, Deut 9:12–21, Deut 32:16–21, Lev 17:1–7, Num 25:1–3, Deut 4:12–25, and Deut 31:16–30 to the theology of the Pentateuch. It has done so in three ways. First, it discussed the intentional connection between Exod 32:7–20 and Deut 9:12–21 and the purposes for that connection. Second, it discussed the innertextuality between the passages and its coherence with the compositional strategies within the Pentateuch. Third, it utilized the results of this analysis in order to contribute to the contemporary expression of the theology of the Pentateuch.

RESULTS AND IMPLICATIONS FOR BIBLICAL STUDIES

This section will discuss the results and implications this analysis has for biblical studies. It will do so by suggesting avenues of further studies between these passages within the Pentateuch and other related passages throughout the Old and New Testaments. It will also suggest directions for further study.

Other passages related to the theme of idolatry and the narratives of the golden calf should be examined for signs of textual relationship. Instances of these occurrences will not be innertextuality *per se* but rather occasions of allusion or intertextuality.[2] Passages to be included in an examination could include 1 Kings 9, 12; Psalm 78; Hosea 1–3; 2 Chronicles 8, 13, 25, 34; Acts 7, and 1 Corinthians 10.

The innertextuality in this analysis shows the severity of Israel's apostasy and the development of that theme throughout the Pentateuch. As a result of Israel's apostasy, God makes Israel jealous with "not a people" (Deut 32:21). In consideration of these themes, passages related to the innertexts demonstrated in this analysis should be examined for signs of allusion and continuity with these themes.

Hosea 1:9; 2:1; and 2:25 appear to be allusions to Deut 32:16–21. Old Testament scholars acknowledge that 1 Kgs 12:28 relates to Exodus 32.[3] Psalm 78 rehearses a history of the Israelite people and comments on their idolatrous ways. Likewise, Acts 7 rehearses a history of the Israelite people and alludes to the golden calf. First Corinthians 10 points to Israel and maintains they were worshipping demons. All these passages in some manner show signs of relating to the innertexts in this analysis. Using criteria of association, examinations can be accomplished which establish the manner of relationship and the purposed behind that relationship.

Another avenue for further study involves the pursuit of other themes in the Pentateuch which are related in an innertextual manner. The compositional strategies within the Pentateuch can be registered and noted for their contribution to a theology of the Pentateuch. The resulting strategies can be examined for their proper coherence and prominence in a theology of the Pentateuch.

Another avenue for further study involves the criteria of association. Additional study of texts may establish distinct criteria. These criteria would not only provide further evidence of an intentional relationship but could be used to rank an order of importance in the criteria and the extent to which each criterion establishes an intentional connection.

This section has discussed the results and implications this analysis has for biblical studies. It has accomplished this by suggesting avenues of further studies between these passages within the Pentateuch and other related passages throughout the Old and New Testaments. It has also suggested avenues for further study related to different innertextual themes and passages within the Pentateuch. Lastly, it has suggested that additional

2. Sailhamer, *Introduction to Old Testament Theology*, 212–13.
3. Schmitt, "Erzählung vom Goldenen Kalb," 237–49.

analyses would contribute to the number of criteria and to the extent to which the criteria establish an intentional connection.

Bibliography

Alter, Robert. *The Art of Biblical Narrative*. New York: Basic Books, 1981.

Archer, Gleason L., Jr. *A Survey of Old Testament Introduction*. Chicago: Moody, 1964.

Aurelius, Erik. *Der Fürbitter Israels: Eine Studie Zum Mosebild Im Alten Testament*. ConBOT 27. Stockholm: Almquist & Wiksell International, 1988.

Bar-Efrat, Shimeon. *Narrative Art in the Bible*. Bible and Literature Series 17. Sheffield: Almond, 1989.

————. "Some Observations on the Analysis of Structure in Biblical Narrative." *VT* 30 (1980) 154–73.

Barton, John. *Reading the Old Testament: Method in Biblical Study*. 2nd ed. London: Darton, Longman & Todd, 1996.

Becker, Uwe. *Exegese des Alten Testaments: Ein Methoden- Und Arbeitsbuch*. UTB 2664. Tübingen: Mohr/Siebeck, 2005.

Begg, Christopher T. "The Destruction of the Calf (Exod 32,20 and Deut 9,21)." In *Deuteronomium: Entstehung, Gestalt und Botschaf*, 208–51. BETL 68. Leuven: Peeters, 1985.

————. "The Destruction of the Golden Calf Revisited (Exod 32,20/Deut 9,21)." In *Deuteronomy and Deuteronomic Literature: Festschrift: C. H. W. Brekelmans*, 469–79. BETL 133. Leuven: Peeters, 1997.

Ben-Porat, Ziva. "The Poetics of Literary Allusion." *PTL: A Journal for Descriptive Poetics and Theory of Literature* 1 (1976) 105–28.

Bendavid, Abba. *Parallels in the Bible*. Jerusalem: Carta, 1972.

Bibleworks. Bibleworks LLC, Norfolk, VA.

Biddle, Mark E. *Deuteronomy*. Smyth & Helwys Bible Commentary 4. Macon, GA: Smyth & Helwys, 2003.

Boorer, Suzanne. *The Promise of the Land as Oath: A Key to the Formation of the Pentateuch*. BZAW 205. Berlin: de Gruyter, 1992.

Brown, Francis, et al. *The Brown-Driver-Briggs Hebrew and English Lexicon*. Peabody, MA: Hendrickson, 1996.

Cassuto, Umberto. *Biblical and Oriental Studies*. Vol. 1, *The Bible*. Translated by Israel Abrahams. Jerusalem: Magnes, 1973.

————. *A Commentary on the Book of Exodus*. Translated by Israel Abrahams. Publications of the Perry Foundation for Biblical Research in the Hebrew University of Jerusalem. Jerusalem: Magnes, 1968.

————. *The Documentary Hypothesis and the Composition of the Pentateuch: Eight Lectures*. Translated by Israel Abrahams. Jerusalem: Magnes, 1961.

Chandler, James K. "Romantic Allusiveness." *Critical Inquiry* 8 (1982) 461–87.

Charlesworth, James H. "Intertextuality: Isaiah 40:3 and the *Serek Ha-Yahad*." In *The Quest for Context and Meaning: Studies in Biblical Intertextuality in Honor of James A.*

Sanders, edited by Craig A. Evans, et al., 197–224. Biblical Interpretation Series 28. Leiden: Brill, 1997.

Childs, Brevard S. *Biblical Theology in Crisis*. Philadelphia: Westminster, 1970.

———. *The Book of Exodus: A Critical, Theological Commentary*. OTL. Philadelphia: Westminster, 1974.

———. *Introduction to the Old Testament as Scripture*. Philadelphia: Fortress, 1979.

Clarke, Ernest G., translator. *Targum Pseudo-Jonathan: Deuteronomy*. The Aramaic Bible 58. Collegeville, MN: Liturgical, 1998.

Crüsemann, Frank. "Die Eigenständigkeit der Urgeschichte. Ein Beitrag zur Diskussion um den "Jahwisten." In *Die Botschaft und die Boten: Festschrift für Hans Walter Wolff zum 70. Geburtstag*, edited by Hans Walter Wolff, et al., 11–29. Neukirchen-Vluyn: Neukirchener, 1981.

Dillard, Raymond B., and Tremper Longman III. *An Introduction to the Old Testament*. Grand Rapids: Zondervan, 1994.

Dozeman, Thomas. "The Composition of Ex 32 within the Context of the Enneateuch." In *Auf dem Weg zur Endgestalt von Genesis bis II Regum: Festchrift Hans-Christoph Schmitt zum 65. Geburtstag*, edited by Martin Beck and Ulrike Schorn, 175–89. BZAW 370. Berlin: de Gruyter, 2006.

Driver, S. R. *A Critical and Exegetical Commentary on Deuteronomy*. New York: Scribner, 1903.

Eissfeldt, Otto. "Die Kleinste Literarische Einheit in den Erzählungsbüchern des Alten Testaments." In *Kleine Schriften* 1:143–49. Tübingen: Mohr/Siebeck, 1962.

Engnell, Ivan. "Methodological Aspects of Old Testament Study." In *Congress Volume, Oxford, 1959*, 13–30. VTSup 7. Leiden: Brill, 1960.

Even-Shoshan, Abraham, editor. *A New Concordance of the Bible*. 3 vols. in 4 bks. Jerusalem: Kiryat Sefer, 1993.

Exum, J. Cheryl, and David J. A. Clines, editors. *The New Literary Criticism and the Hebrew Bible*. JSOTSup 143. Sheffield: JSOT Press, 1993.

Farrar, Frederic William. *History of Interpretation*. Bampton Lectures. London: Macmillan, 1886.

Fishbane, Michael A. *Biblical Interpretation in Ancient Israel*. Oxford: Clarendon, 1985.

Fohrer, Georg. *Exegese des Alten Testaments: Einführung in die Methodik*. 6th ed. UTB 267. Heidelberg: Quelle und Meyer, 1993.

Fowler, Alastair. *Kinds of Literature: An Introduction to the Theory of Genres and Modes*. Cambridge: Harvard University Press, 1982.

Freedman, Harry, and Maurice Simon, editors and translators. *Midrash Rabbah*. 3rd ed. New York: Soncino, 1983.

Friedman, Richard Elliott. *The Bible with Sources Revealed: A New View into the Five Books of Moses*. 1st ed. San Francisco: HarperSanFrancisco, 2003.

Gesenius, Wilhelm, et al. *Gesenius' Hebrew Grammar*. Edited and enlarged by the late Emil Kautzsch. 2nd Eng. ed. Oxford: Clarendon, 1983.

Ginsburger, Moses. *Pseudo-Jonathan (Thargum Jonathan Ben Usiel zum Pentateuch)*. 1903. Reprinted, Hildesheim: Olms, 1971.

Grossberg, Daniel. "The Disparate Elements of the Inclusio in Psalms." *Hebrew Annual* (1982) 97–104.

Gunkel, Hermann. *Genesis*. Translated by Mark E. Biddle. Mercer Library of Biblical Studies. Macon, GA: Mercer University Press, 1997.

Bibliography

————. *The Legends of Genesis, the Biblical Saga and History.* Translated by William H. Carruth. New York: Schocken, 1964.

Gunkel, Hermann, and Heinrich Zimmern. *Schöpfung und Chaos in Urzeit und Endzeit: Eine Religionsgeschichtliche Untersuchung über Gen 1 und Ap Joh 12.* Göttingen: Vandenhoeck & Ruprecht, 1895.

Hahn, Joachim. *Das "Goldene Kalb": Die Jahwe-Verehrung bei Stierbildern in der Geschichte Israels.* Europäische Hochschulschriften. Reihe XXIII, Theologie. Bd. 154 Frankfurt: Lang, 1981.

Hartley, John E. *Leviticus.* WBC 4. Dallas: Word, 1992.

Hauge, Martin Ravndal. *The Descent from the Mountain: Narrative Patterns in Exodus 19–40.* JSOTSup 323. Sheffield: Sheffield Academic, 2001.

Hayes, Christine Elizabeth. "Golden Calf Stories: The Relationship of Exodus 32 and Deuteronomy 9–10." In *The Idea of Biblical Interpretation: Essays in Honor of James L. Kugel,* edited by Hindy Najman and Judith H. Newman. 45–93. JSJSup 83. Leiden: Brill, 2004.

Hays, Richard B. *Echoes of Scripture in the Letters of Paul.* New Haven: Yale University Press, 1989.

Hayward, Robert, and Michael Maher. *Targum Pseudo-Jonathan: Exodus.* Aramaic Bible 2. Collegeville, MN: Liturgical, 1994.

Hertzberg, Hans Wilhelm. "Die Nachgeschichte Alttestamentlicher Texte Innerhalb des Alten Testaments." In *Werden und Wesen des Alten Testaments,* edited by Paul Volz, et al., 110–21. BZAW 66. Berlin: Töpelmann, 1936.

————. "Ist Exegese Theologisch Möglich?" In *Beiträge zur Traditions-geschichte und Theologie des Alten Testaments,* 101–17. Göttingen: Vandenhoeck & Ruprecht, 1962.

Hirsch, E. D. *Validity in Interpretation.* New Haven: Yale University Press, 1967.

Hurvitz, Avi. *A Linguistic Study of the Relationship between the Priestly Source and the Book of Ezekiel: A New Approach to an Old Problem* CahRB 20. Paris: Gabalda, 1982.

Hyatt, J. Philip. *Commentary on Exodus.* NCB. London: Oliphants, 1971.

Jastrow, Marcus. *A Dictionary of the Targumim, the Talmud Babli and Yerushalmi, and the Midrashic Literature.* 2 vols. 1903. Reprinted, Peabody, MA: Hendrickson, 2005.

Jerome. *Opera.* CCSL 74. Turnholti: Typographi Brepols, 1960.

Joo, Samantha. *Provocation and Punishment: The Anger of God in the Book of Jeremiah and Deuteronomistic Theology.* BZAW 361. Berlin: de Gruyter, 2006.

Kaufmann, Yehezkel. *The Religion of Israel, from Its Beginnings to the Babylonian Exile.* Translated and abridged by Moshe Greenberg. Chicago: University of Chicago Press, 1960.

Keil, Carl Friedrich, and Franz Delitzsch. *Biblical Commentary on the Old Testament.* Vol. 2. Peabody, MA: Hendrickson, 1996.

Kittel, Rudolf, et al. *Torah, Nevi'im uKetuvim = Biblia Hebraica Stuttgartensia.* 5th ed. Stuttgart: Deutsche Bibelgesellschaft, 1997.

Klostermann, A. "Beiträge zur Entstehungsgeschichte des Pentateuchs." *ZTK* 38 (1877) 401–5.

Knierim, Rolf P. "The Composition of the Pentateuch." *SBLSP* 24 (1985) 393–415.

Kochavi, M., et al. *Aphek-Antipatris, 1974–1977: The Inscriptions.* Vol. 2. Reprint Series–Journal of the Tel Aviv University Institute of Archaeology. Tel Aviv: Tel Aviv University, Institute of Archaeology, 1978.

Kratz, Reinhard Gregor. "Redaktionsgeschichte-Redaktionskritik." In *TRE* 28:367–78, 1997.

Kratz, Reinhard Gregor, et al. *Schriftauslegung in der Schrift: Festschrift für Odil Hannes Steck zu Seinem 65. Geburtstag.* BZAW 300. Berlin: de Gruyter, 2000.

Kronfeld, Chana. "Allusion: An Israeli Perspective." *Prooftexts* 5 (1985) 137–63.

Lawson, Ian. "The Literary Relationship between Deuteronomy 30:1–10 and Ezekiel 36:22–32." MA thesis, Trinity Evangelical Divinity School, 1985.

Levin, Christoph. *Der Jahwist.* FRLANT 157. Göttingen: Vandenhoeck & Ruprecht, 1993.

Lindqvist, Pekka. *Sin at Sinai: Early Judaism Encounters Exodus 32.* Studies in Rewritten Bible 2. Winona Lake: Eisenbrauns, 2008.

Loewenstamm, Samuel E. "Making and Destruction of the Golden Calf." *Biblica* 48 (1967) 481–91.

———. "Making and Destruction of the Golden Calf: A Rejoinder." *Bib* 56 (1975) 330–43.

Lohfink, Norbert. *Das Hauptgebot: Eine Untersuchung Literarischer Einleitungsfragen zu Dtn 5–11.* AnBib 20. Rome: E. Pontificio Instituto Biblico, 1963.

Longenecker, Richard N. *Biblical Exegesis in the Apostolic Period.* 2nd ed. Grand Rapids: Eerdmans, 1999.

McCann, J. Clinton, Jr. "Exodus 32:1–14." *Int* 44 (1990) 277–81.

McKenzie, Steven L., and Thomas Römer, editors; in collaboration with Hans Heinrich Schmid. *Rethinking the Foundations: Historiography in the Ancient World and in the Bible: Essays in Honour of John Van Seters.* BZAW 294. Berlin: de Gruyter, 2000.

McNamara, Martin. *Targum Neofiti 1: Deuteronomy.* Translated with an apparatus by Martin McNamera. Aramaic Bible 5A. Collegeville, MN: Liturgical, 1997.

McNamara, Martin, et al. *Targum Neofiti 1: Leviticus.* Translated with an apparatus by Martin McNamera. Aramaic Bible 3. Collegeville, MN: Liturgical, 1994.

Meadors, Edward P. *Idolatry and the Hardening of the Heart: A Study in Biblical Theology.* London: T. & T. Clark, 2006.

Mettinger, T. N. D. "Intertextuality: Allusion and Vertical Context Systems in Some Job Passages." In *Of Prophets' Visions and the Wisdom of Sages: Essays in Honour of R. Norman Whybray on His Seventieth Birthday,* edited by R. N. Whybray, et al., 257–80. JSOTSup 162. Sheffield: JSOT Press, 1993.

Mikra'ot Gedolot. Tel-Aviv: Pardes, [1969] 1954–1957.

Miller, Patrick D. *The Religion of Ancient Israel.* Library of Ancient Israel. Louisville: Westminster John Knox Press, 2000.

Muilenburg, James. "Form Criticism and Beyond." *JBL* 88 (1969) 1–18.

Nielsen, Kirsten. "Intertextuality and Hebrew Bible." In *Congress Volume: Oslo 1998,* edited by André Lemaire and Sæbø Magne, 17–31. VTSup 80. Leiden: Brill, 2000.

Noble, Paul R. "Esau, Tamar, and Joseph: Criteria for Identifying Inner-Biblical Allusions." *VT* 52 (2002) 219–52.

Noth, Martin. *Exodus: A Commentary.* Translated by J. S. Bowden. OTL. Philadelphia: Westminster, 1962.

———. *Leviticus: A Commentary.* Translated by J. E. Anderson. Rev. ed. OTL. Philadelphia: Westminster, 1977.

O'Connell, Robert H. "Deuteronomy viii 1–20: Asymmetrical Concentricity and the Rhetoric of Providence." *VT* 40 (1990) 437–52.

———. "Deuteronomy IX 7—X 7, 10–11: Panelled Structure, Double Rehearsal and the Rhetoric of Covenant Rebuke." *VT* 42 (1992) 492–509.

Olson, Dennis T. *Deuteronomy and the Death of Moses: A Theological Reading.* OBT. Minneapolis: Fortress, 1994.

Bibliography

Origen. *Commentary on the Epistle to the Romans. Books 1–5.* Translated by Thomas P. Scheck. Fathers of the Church 103. Washington, DC: Catholic University of America Press, 2001.

Perri, Carmela. "On Alluding." *Poetics* 7 (1978) 289–307.

Pratico, Gary Davis, and Miles V. Van Pelt. *Basics of Biblical Hebrew Grammar.* Grand Rapids: Zondervan, 2001.

Rad, Gerhard von. *Old Testament Theology.* Vol. 2, *The Theology of Israel's Prophetic Traditions.* Translated by D. M. G. Stalker. New York: Harper & Row, 1965.

————. *Wisdom in Israel.* Translated by James D. Martin. Nashville: Abingdon, 1972.

Rahlfs, Alfred, editor. *Septuaginta: Id Est, Vetus Testamentum Graece Iuxta LXX Interpretes.* 2 vols. in 1. Editio minor. Stuttgart: Deutsche Bibelgesellschaft, 1979.

Reasoner, Mark. "The Relationship of Three Old Testament Woman-at-the-Well Texts to John 4:1–42." MA thesis, Trinity Evangelical Divinity School, 1985.

Rendtorff, Rolf. *The Canonical Hebrew Bible: A Theology of the Old Testament.* Translated by David E. Orton. Tools for Biblical Studies Series 7. Leiden: Deo, 2005.

————. "How to Read the Book of the Twelve as a Theological Unity." In *Reading and Hearing the Book of the Twelve,* edited by James D. Nogalski and Marvin A. Sweeney, 75–87. SBLSymS 15. Atlanta: Society of Biblical Literature, 2000.

————. *Leviticus.* Vol. 1. 3 vols. BKAT. Neukirchen-Vluyn: Neukirchener, 1985.

————. "Literarkritik und Traditionsgeschichte." *EvT* 27 (1967) 138–53.

————. "Traditio-Historical Method and the Documentary Hypothesis." In *Proceedings of the Fifth World Congress of Jewish Studies.* Vol. 1, *The Ancient Near East Related to the Bible and the Holy Land,* 5–11. Pirsume ha-Igud ha-'olami le-mada'e ha-Yahadut. Jerusalem: Hacohen, 1969.

————. *The Problem of the Process of Transmission in the Pentateuch.* Translated by John J. Scullion. JSOTSup 89. Sheffield: JSOT Press, 1990.

————. *Das überlieferungsgeschichtliche Problem des Pentateuch.* BZAW 147. Berlin: de Gruyter, 1977.

————. "The 'Yahwist' As Theologian: Dilemma of Pentateuchal Criticism." *JSOT* 3 (1977) 2–45.

Rogerson, J. W. *Old Testament Criticism in the Nineteenth Century: England and Germany.* Philadelphia: Fortress, 1985.

Rooker, Mark F. *Leviticus.* NAC 3A. Nashville: Broadman & Holman, 2000.

Rosenberg, A. J. *Shemoth (The Book of Exodus).* Judaica Press Books of the Bible 1. New York: Judaica Press, 1995.

Sailhamer, John H. "Biblical Theology and the Composition of the Hebrew Bible." In *Biblical Theology: Retrospect and Prospect,* edited by Scott J. Hafemann, 25–37. Downers Grove, IL: InterVarsity, 2002.

————. "Hosea 11:1 and Matthew 2:15." *WTJ* 63 (2001) 87–96.

————. *Introduction to Old Testament Theology: A Canonical Approach.* Grand Rapids: Zondervan, 1995.

————. *The Pentateuch as Narrative: A Biblical-Theological Commentary.* Library of Biblical Interpretation. Grand Rapids: Zondervan, 1992.

Sandmel, Samuel. "Haggada within Scripture." *JBL* 80 (1961) 105–22.

Sarna, Nahum M. *Exodus = [Shemot]: The Traditional Hebrew Text with the New JPS Translation.* 1st ed. The JPS Torah Commentary. Philadelphia: Jewish Publication Society, 1991.

Scharbert, Josef. *Exodus.* NEchtB. Kommentar zum Alten Testament mit der Einheits-übersetzung 24. Würzburg: Echter, 1989.

Schmid, Konrad. "Innerbiblische Schriftauslegung. Aspekte der Forschungsgeschichte." In *Schriftauslegung in der Schrift: Festschrift für Odil Hannes Steck zu Seinem 65. Geburtstag,* edited by Reinhard Gregor Kratz, 1–22. BZAW 300. Berlin: de Gruyter, 2000.

Schmitt, Hans-Christoph. "Review of *Genesis und Exodus* by C. F. Keil." *ZAW* 96 (1984) 457.

———. "Die Erzählung vom Goldenen Kalb Ex. 32* und Das Deuteronomistische Geschichtswerk." In *Rethinking the Foundations: Historiography in the Ancient World and in the Bible; Essays in Honour of John Van Seeters,* edited by Steven L. McKenzie and Thomas Römer, in collaboration with Hans Heinrich Schmid, 235–50. BZAW 294. Berlin: de Gruyter, 2000.

———. "Redaktion des Pentateuch im Geiste der Prophetie : Zur Bedeutung der "Glaubens"-Thematik Innerhalb der Theologie des Pentateuch." *VT* 32 (1982) 170–89.

Schneider, Wolfgang. *Grammatik des biblischen Hebräisch: Ein Lehrbuch.* 2nd ed. Munich: Claudius, 2004.

Schniedewind, William M. *How the Bible Became a Book: The Textualization of Ancient Israel.* Cambridge: Cambridge University Press, 2004.

Schultz, Richard L. *The Search for Quotation: Verbal Parallels in the Prophets.* JSOTSup 180. Sheffield: Sheffield Academic, 1999.

Schwartz, Baruch J. "'Profane' Slaughter and the Integrity of the Priestly Code." *Hebrew Union College Annual* 67 (1996) 15–42.

Seeligmann, I. L. "Voraussetzungen der Midraschexegese." In *Congress Volume, Copenhagen, 1953,* 150–81. VTSup 1. Leiden: Brill, 1953.

Seitz, Christopher R. "On Letting a Text 'Act Like a Man'—The Book of the Twelve: New Horizons for Canonical Reading, with Hermeneutical Reflections." *SBET* 22 (2004) 159–76.

Smith, George Adam. *The Book of the Twelve Prophets, Commonly Called the Minor.* 2 vols. The Expositor's Bible. Minor Prophets. New York: George H. Doran, (1898).

Snaith, Norman Henry. "The Meaning of םיריעש." *VT* 25 (1975) 115–18.

———. "Verbs *Zabah* and *Sahat.*" *VT* 25 (1975) 242–46.

Sommer, Benjamin D. "Exegesis, Allusion and Intertextuality in the Hebrew Bible: A Response to Lyle Eslinger." *VT* 46 (1996) 479–89.

———. *A Prophet Reads Scripture: Allusion in Isaiah 40–66.* Contraversions: Jews and Other Differences. Stanford: Stanford University Press, 1998.

Sparks, Kenton L. *Ancient Texts for the Study of the Hebrew Bible: A Guide to Background Literature.* Peabody, MA: Hendrickson, 2005.

Spinoza, Benedictus de. *A Theologico-Political Treatise and a Political Treatise.* Translated by R. H. M. Elwes. New York: Dover, 1951.

Stackert, Jeffery. "Why Does Deuteronomy Legislate Cities of Refuge? Asylum in the Covenant Collection (Exodus 21:12–14) and Deuteronomy (19:1–13)." *JBL* 125 (2006) 23–49.

Talstra, E. "Deuteronomy 9 and 10: Synchronic and Diachronic Observations." In *Synchronic or Diachronic? A Debate on Method in Old Testament Exegesis,* edited by Johannes C. de Moor, 187–210. OtSt 34. Leiden: Brill, 1995.

Bibliography

Thiselton, Anthony C. *New Horizons in Hermeneutics: The Theory and Practice of Transforming Biblical Reading.* Grand Rapids: Zondervan, 1992.

Thompson, R. J. *Moses and the Law in a Century of Criticism since Graf.* VTSup 19. Leiden: Brill, 1970.

Trattner, Ernest R. *Unravelling the Book of Books: Being the Story of How the Puzzles of the Bible Were Solved, and Its Documents Unravelled.* New York: Scribner's, 1929.

Van Seters, John. "An Ironic Circle: Wellhausen and the Rise of Redaction Criticism." *ZAW* 115 (2003) 487–500.

————. *The Life of Moses: The Yahwist as Historian in Exodus-Numbers.* 1st ed. Louisville: Westminster John Knox, 1994.

————. *Prologue to History: The Yahwist as Historian in Genesis.* 1st ed. Louisville: Westminster John Knox, 1992.

————. "The Redactor in Biblical Studies: A Nineteenth Century Anachronism." *JNSL* 29 (2003) 1–19.

Venema, G. J. *Reading Scripture in the Old Testament: Deuteronomy 9–10, 31, 2 Kings 22–23, Jeremiah 36, Nehemiah 8.* OtSt 48. Leiden: Brill, 2004.

Vervenne, Marc, and Johan Lust. *Deuteronomy and Deuteronomic Literature: Festschrift C. H. W. Brekelmans.* BETL 133 Leuven: Peeters, 1997.

Volz, Paul. *Das Dämonische in Jahwe.* Sammlung gemeinverständlicher Vorträge und Schriften aus dem Gebiet der Theologie und Religionsgeschichte 110. Tübingen: Mohr/Siebeck, 1924.

Wellhausen, Julius. *Prolegomena to the History of Ancient Israel.* Meridian Library 6. New York: Meridian, 1957.

Whybray, Roger N. *The Making of the Pentateuch: A Methodological Study.* JSOTSup 53. Sheffield: JSOT Press, 1987.

Witte, Markus. *Die Biblische Urgeschichte: Redaktions- und Theologiegeschichtliche Beobachtungen zu Genesis 1:1—11:26.* BZAW 265. Berlin: de Gruyter, 1998.

Wynn-Williams, Damian J. *The State of the Pentateuch: A Comparison of the Approaches of M Noth and E Blum.* BZAW 249 Berlin: de Gruyter, 1997.

Zipor, Moshe A. "The Deuteronomic Account of the Golden Calf and Its Reverberation in Other Parts of the Book of Deuteronomy." *ZAW* (1996) 20–33.